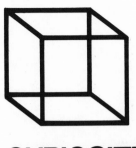

CURIOSITIES
OF THE CUBE

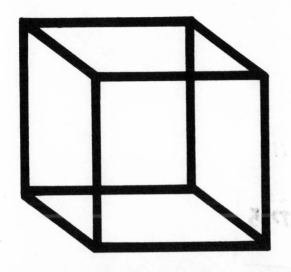

CURIOSITIES OF THE CUBE

ERNEST R. RANUCCI
WILMA E. ROLLINS

ILLUSTRATED BY HENRY ROTH

THOMAS Y. CROWELL COMPANY, NEW YORK

Library of Congress Cataloging in Publication Data
Ranucci, Ernest R. Curiosities of the cube.

   SUMMARY: Includes chapters on putting together and
dissecting cubes, cross sections, geometry of the cube,
games, and curiosities.
   1. Cube—Juv. lit.   [1. Cube.   2. Geometry]
I. Rollins, Wilma E., joint author.   II. Roth, Henry
III. Title.
QA491.R36   516'.23   76-1837
ISBN 0-690-01135-0

1 2 3 4 5 6 7 8 9 10

To Barbara and Carlton

CONTENTS

Preface

From the time when an individual first plays with blocks, he develops a feeling for the space figure called the "cube." As he becomes more sophisticated geometrically, his attention is drawn to a further analysis of the cube. It is amazing that a configuration so simple should be so rich in its possibilities.

The purpose of this book is to make available under one cover much of the wealth of information about the cube. Part of the collection requires some mathematical sophistication, although computation has been kept to a minimum. Stress is placed on the use of visualization and imagination in carrying out investigations. It is the hope of the authors to further in the reader the sense of wonder, for:

"Wonder is the feeling of a philosopher, and philosophy begins with wonder."

Socrates in Plato's *Theaetatus*

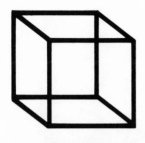

CURIOSITIES
OF THE CUBE

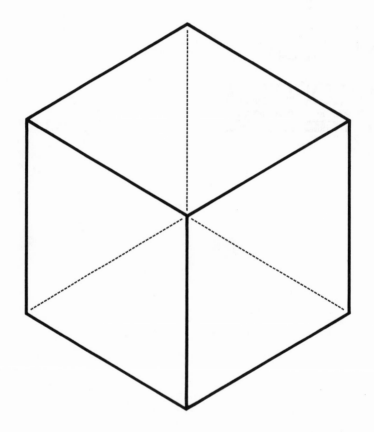

Fig. 1–1

CHAPTER I
Cues on Cubes

In the simplest possible terms, the shape commonly called a "cube" is like a baby's block. But a cube is much more than that.

Throughout this book we shall consider this figure in terms of its geometry. The six faces of a cube, all squares, meet each other at twelve edges. The geometer calls these edges "line segments." These twelve edges meet each other in eight corners. The geometer calls these "vertices."

More formally, a cube is a space figure bounded by six congruent squares (Fig. 1–1). Since each square is itself bounded by four equal edges, you may think, at first, that the total number of edges in a cube would be 6×4, or 24. But each edge is shared by two adjacent squares. Thus the total number of edges is, in fact, $24 \div 2$, or 12, as stated above.

The same sort of problem about edges occurs when the vertices of the cube are examined. Three edges meet at each of the eight vertices of the cube. You might expect the total number of edges to be 24, *i.e.,* 8×3. But each edge is still shared by two adjacent squares. The total number of edges remains 12, *i.e.,* $24 \div 2$.

Any edge of a cube is identical with any other edge. Unless the edges are colored differently or identified in some other way, you cannot tell them apart (Fig. 1–2).

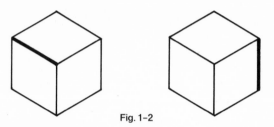

Fig. 1–2

There is a limited number of ways in which *two* edges can be related to each other. If any two of the twelve edges of a cube are selected, three basic relationships can arise:

    1. The two edges may be parallel (Fig. 1–3).
    2. The two edges may intersect (Fig. 1–4).
    3. The two edges may be skew. Skew lines never meet. Unlike parallel lines, they do not lie in the same plane (Fig. 1–5).

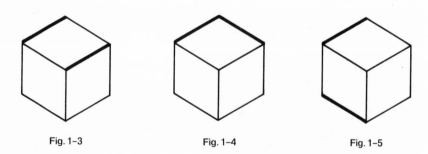

Fig. 1–3   Fig. 1–4   Fig. 1–5

In Case 1, two possibilities actually arise. The two parallel edges can have a perpendicular distance between them

2

of either e (the length of an edge) or $e\sqrt{2}$ (the length of the diagonal of a square) (Fig. 1–6).

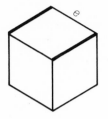 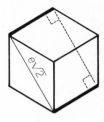

Fig. 1–6

Only one possible relation can exist in Case 2. Any two intersecting edges must be perpendicular to each other.

In Case 3, any two skew edges must be "perpendicular" to each other. The reason for the quotation marks is that the lines are not literally perpendicular. After all, they do not actually meet. They are called "perpendicular" because, by definition, the angle between skew lines is the angle between their projections on each other.

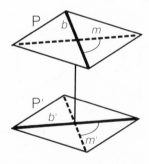

Fig. 1–7

In Fig. 1–7, b and b' are skew lines; m' is the projection (shadow) of b onto the plane P' and m is the projection (shadow) of b' onto the plane P. The projection m is parallel to b', and m' is parallel to b. The angles between b and m and b' and m' are equal.

3

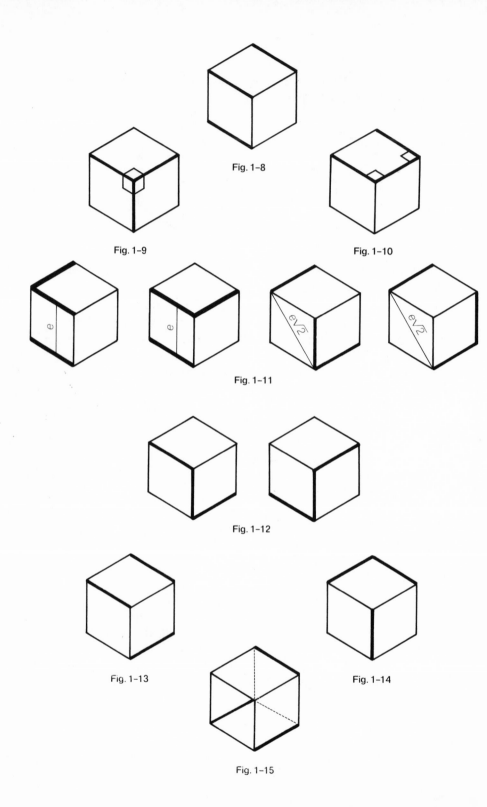

Fig. 1-8

Fig. 1-9

Fig. 1-10

Fig. 1-11

Fig. 1-12

Fig. 1-13

Fig. 1-14

Fig. 1-15

Three of the 12 edges of a cube can relate in more numerous ways. The following possibilities exist:

1. The three edges may be parallel (Fig. 1–8).

2. The three edges may be concurrent. Concurrent lines always pass through some common point (Fig. 1–9).

3. The three edges may be coplanar. Coplanar lines always lie in the same plane (Fig. 1–10). Two of the edges will be perpendicular to the third. The two edges will also be parallel to each other.

4. Two edges may be perpendicular to each other. The third may be parallel to one of the original two. There are two basic cases here, but mirror-image possibilities make it look like four. The parallel lines involved are at a distance of either $e \sqrt{2}$ or e (Fig. 1–11).

5. Two edges may be skew segments with a common perpendicular (Fig. 1–12). Here again, mirror images are involved.

6. Two edges may be parallel. The third may be skew to both of them (Fig. 1–13).

7. Two edges may be perpendicular to each other. The third may be perpendicular to the plane of the two (Fig. 1–14).

8. The three edges may all be skew to one another (Fig. 1–15).

When it comes to the selection of four, five, six, seven or more edges of the original twelve, the relationships become quite complicated. Perhaps you can explore these possibilities. We *do* know that there is but one possibility for the selection of twelve edges. . . .

The discussions so far may suggest that there is more to a cube than meets the eye. How much more there is should become apparent in the remaining chapters.

CHAPTER II
Putting Cubes Together

Cube Folding

There are eleven basic patterns of six squares that can be folded to form a cube (see Fig. 2–1). In each of these patterns, faces that are not parallel to each other have been marked A, B and C. Locate A′, the face that is parallel to A on the original cube. In a similar manner, locate B′ and C′.

Flaps for gluing would have to be provided for each of the eleven patterns of the cube if the cubes were actually to be constructed. In each of the eleven patterns provide a possible set of flaps. Is the number of such flaps constant for all eleven patterns?

The Japanese technique of paper folding, *origami,* provides an interesting way of making a cube from an ordinary piece of paper.

Start with a square piece of paper—the larger, the better (Fig. 2–2a). Crease it on the diagonals (Fig. 2–2b). Crease it

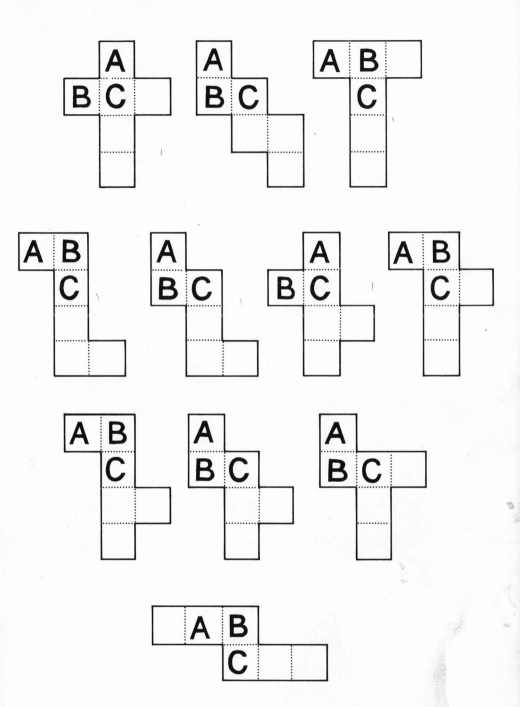

Fig. 2-1. Patterns of the Surfaces of a Cube.

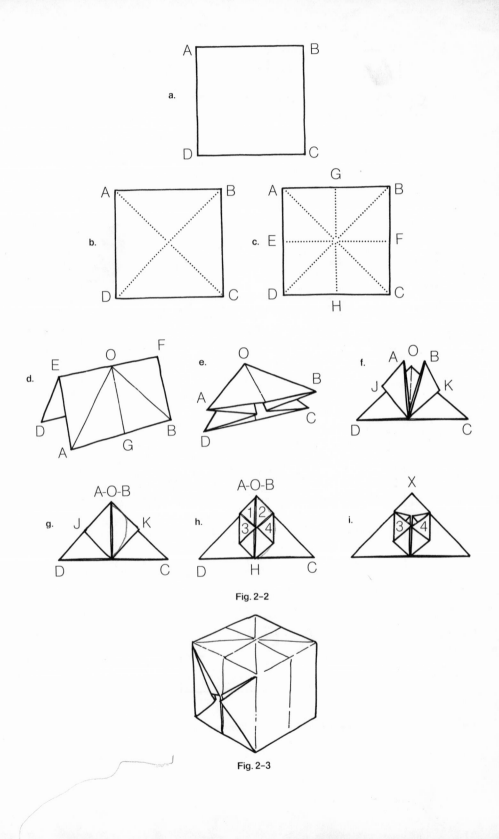

Fig. 2-2

Fig. 2-3

on the vertical, then the horizontal (Fig. 2–2c). Fold **AB** down on **DC** (Fig. 2–2d). Tuck in on points **E** and **F** (Fig. 2–2e). Fold **A** to **O**; fold **B** to **O** (Fig. 2–2f). Flatten the assembly (Fig. 2–2g). Fold **J** to the center of **OH**; fold **K** to the center of **OH**. Flatten the assembly (Fig. 2–2h). Tuck the flap at 1 *into* the fold at 3; tuck the flap at 2 *into* the fold at 4 (Fig. 2–2i).

Turn the whole assembly over and repeat the directions. Flatten out all the creases.

Now open the assembly and blow slowly and steadily into the opening at **x**. With a little assistance, you will have a cube such as that in Fig. 2–3.

The directions for the folding of this cube were adapted from a newspaper article dated March 22, 1888.

Consider the arrangement of the 14½ squares shown in Fig. 2–4a. These squares can be "braided" in such a way as to form a rigid figure without tabs. Lay out a pattern of one-inch squares and label them as in Fig. 2–4a. Follow Fig. 2–4b–h, finally tucking the half square (O) *under* face A. Be sure to cut on the heavy line indicated in the diagram and start by folding square A *onto* square B.

Cubes can also be constructed by folding strips of paper. Start with a strip that is 7 inches long and 1 inch wide. Mark it off into seven squares. Since it takes only six squares to form the faces of a cube, one square here must be "lost." Crease along the marked edges and the two diagonals as shown in Fig. 2–5a. Fold *up* along diagonal *a* and *down* along diagonal *b* as in Fig. 2–5b. Bring *b* to meet *a* so that they become the diagonal of a face (Fig. 2–5c). Finally, fold faces A and B down to complete the cube (Fig. 2–5d). It may not be easy to hold, but it *is* a cube!

If you would like to be able to hold this cube easily, first place a piece of tape across the diagonals *a* and *b*. A piece of the tape on face A and one on face B, both attached to the face opposite the diagonals, will produce a rigid cube.

Here are two more cubes that can be constructed by fold-ing paper. The first one starts with a rectangle 2 inches by 6

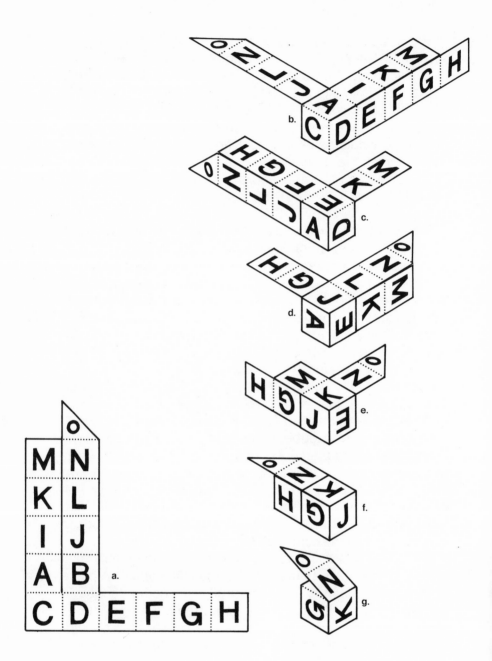

Fig. 2-4

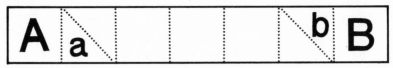

a.

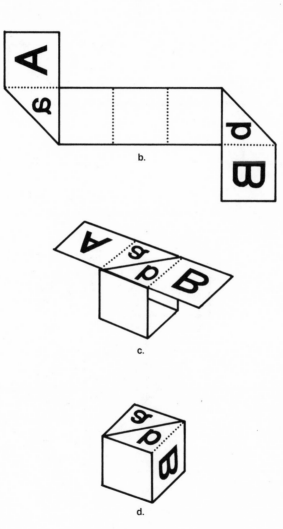

b.

c.

d.

Fig. 2–5

inches marked as shown in Fig. 2–6. Using this pattern, cut along line segments **AB**, **BC** and **CD**. Crease on the remaining line segments. The two pieces can be folded into a cube with no overlapping of edges, but much tape will be needed. Perhaps a starting hint is in order: Match segments *a* and segments *b,* taping as you go.

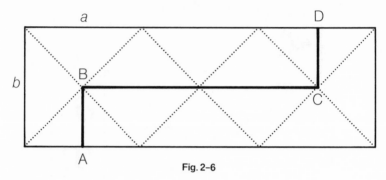

Fig. 2–6

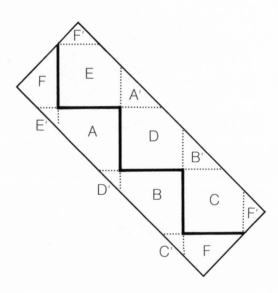

Fig. 2–7

To make the second one, cut the pattern in Fig. 2–7 along the heavy lines and assemble the two pieces to form a cube after carefully creasing all folds. (*Hint:* Match parts marked A and A'.) Each piece can also be used to illustrate the fact that a cross section of a cube *may* be a regular hexagon. Use plenty of tape in assembling.

Figure 2–8 illustrates how the pattern can be laid out conveniently on graph paper.

Constructing a cube from a 3-inch by 3-inch square is the next problem. Start with the square as shown in Fig. 2–9a. Cut on the heavy lines and crease on all other lines. Fold square B onto square A (Fig. 2–9b). Fold square G under square H (Fig. 2–9c). Now fold strip BC up at right angles to strip HFE (Fig. 2–9d). Fold remaining part so that squares F and E are at right angles to square A (Fig. 2–9e). Finally, fold square D down and square C backward in the direction

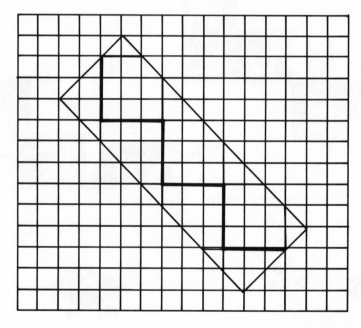

Fig. 2–8

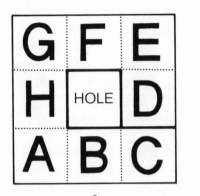

a.

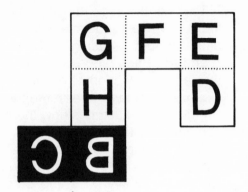

b.

c.

d.

e.

Fig. 2-9

f.

of the arrows. Tape to attach adjacent faces E and F to A and E, and G to C, and D to G will produce a rigid cube, one view of which is shown in Fig. 2–9f.

A Drinking-Straw Construction

The next cube is to be constructed from 12 drinking straws and string. If you wrap the end of the string with a tiny piece of tape and hold the straw perpendicular to the floor, gravity will help "pull" the string through the straw.

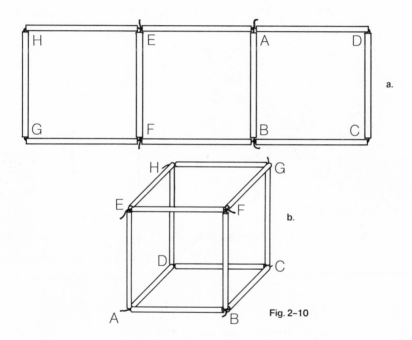

Fig. 2–10

As in Fig. 2–10a start at point **A**, string four straws and knot but do not cut the string. (You are back at **A**.) String three more straws, tie at **B** and cut the string. Attach the string at **F**, put on three straws, tie at **E** and cut. So far the figure will lie in a plane as shown in Fig. 2–10a. Attach the string at **H**, put on one straw, tie at **D** and cut. Attach the string at **G**, put on one straw, tie at **C** and cut. Now you have a cube as shown in Fig. 2–10b.

This cube is certainly not rigid. However, it has possibilities that none of the others have because it can be deformed into many other figures. See if you can deform it into a hexagon, a square, a triangle and a straight-line segment.

Cubes Out of Pyramids

Using Fig. 2–11a as a pattern, cut out and fold up along dotted lines, pasting tabs under the adjacent face. A 2-inch square is a good size. The triangles meeting at **x** are isosceles right triangles; those meeting at **y** would have perpendicular sides 2 inches and $2^7/_8$ inches long, since one is the side of the square and the other is the hypotenuse of the

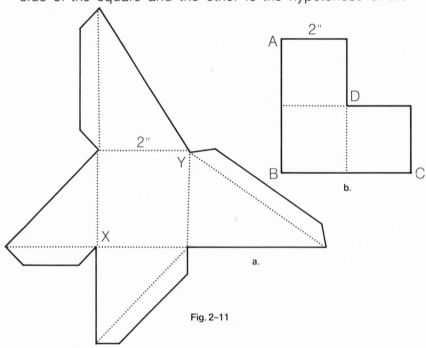

Fig. 2–11

isosceles right triangle with a value of $2\sqrt{2}$. Make three such pyramids and paste them into the pattern shown in Fig. 2–11b. Place x vertices at points A, B and C and Y vertices at D. Bring the vertices of the pyramids together to form the cube.

Make four triangular pyramids using Fig. 2–12a as a pattern. Notice that the base is an equilateral triangle and that each face is an isosceles right triangle. If you make the equilateral triangle 2 inches on each side, the isosceles right triangles are each half a square having a 2-inch diagonal.

Now draw an equilateral triangle with 4-inch sides. Cut it out and crease on the dotted lines before pasting the four pyramids onto it as in Fig. 2–12b.

Fold points A, B and C together to form the cube. Notice that the vertices of the pyramids are four of the vertices of the cube. Where did the other four originate?

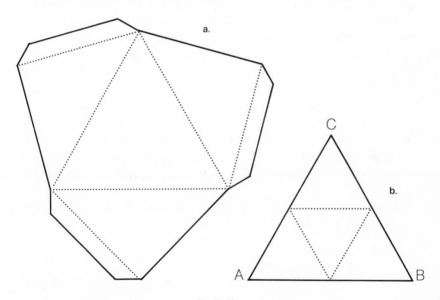

Fig. 2–12

Rhombic Dodecahedron

Constructing the next cube starts with six quadrangular pyramids whose pattern is that of Fig. 2–13. ABCD is a square. The altitude of each triangle is half the length of the diagonal of the square. Lay out six squares, each side the same length as the base of a pyramid, as shown in Fig. 2–14. Paste a pyramid on each square. If you fold so that the pyramids are inside the space figure, you will be holding a cube. If you fold so that the pyramids are on the outside, you will be holding the space figure called a "rhombic dodecahedron" (Fig. 2–15). Its faces are rhombuses, and it has twice as many edges as the cube. The cube is still there, but this time it is on the inside of the figure. Notice that the shorter diagonal of each rhombic face becomes the edge of this cube.

Here is another way to construct a rhombic dodecahedron. Make eight triangular pyramids by using the pattern in Fig. 2–16. To construct one of the small triangles, you need the length of its altitude. Draw a square whose diagonal is the length of a side of the equilateral triangle, say 2 inches. The required altitude is half the length of the side of this square.

Paste the eight pyramids onto the pattern shown in Fig. 2–17. If you fold the resulting figure so that the pyramids are on the inside, you will be holding an octahedron. If you fold so that the pyramids are on the outside, you will be holding the rhombic dodecahedron. The octahedron is still there, but this time it is on the inside.

Notice that the longer diagonal of each rhombic face becomes the edge of this octahedron.

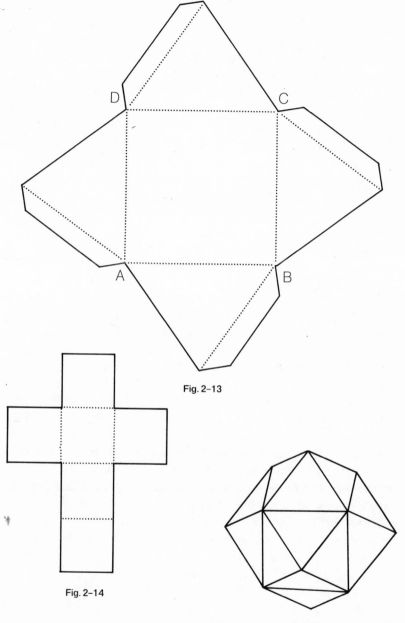

D C

A B

Fig. 2-13

Fig. 2-14

Fig. 2-15

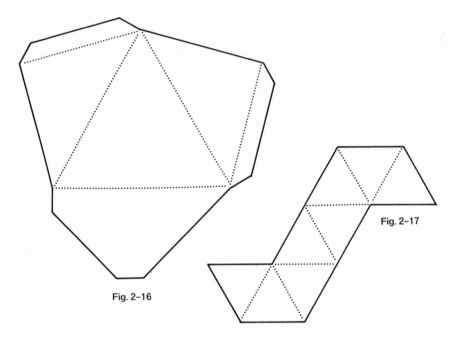

Fig. 2-16

Fig. 2-17

An Octahedron

Associated with the cube is the regular octahedron, its space dual. Duality will be discussed at greater length on p. 67, but it is sufficient here to state that the octahedron may be formed by connecting the center of each face of a cube to the centers of each adjacent face. Hence the centers of the faces of a cube are the vertices of an octahedron. Likewise, the centers of each of the faces of an octahedron are the vertices of a cube.

To construct an octahedron you will need 12 straws and some string, just as you did for the cube on page 15. This time, cut a piece of string about 14 times as long as a straw to allow for tying and wrapping, as this time the string will not have to be cut. Follow Fig. 2–18a–g, leaving about 3 inches of string at the starting point to make it easier to tie the strings at the finish. The small square indicates vertices

20

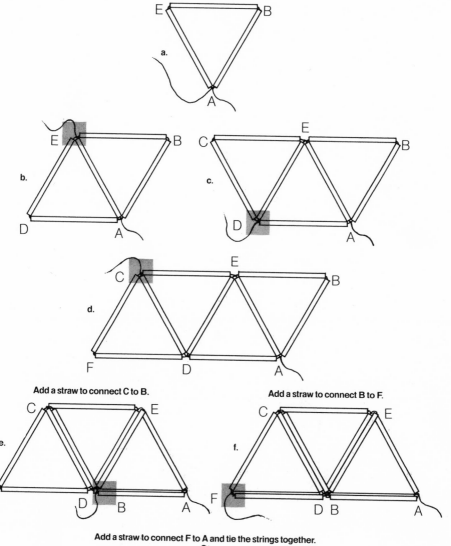

Add a straw to connect C to B.

Add a straw to connect B to F.

Add a straw to connect F to A and tie the strings together.

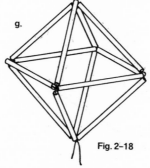

Fig. 2–18

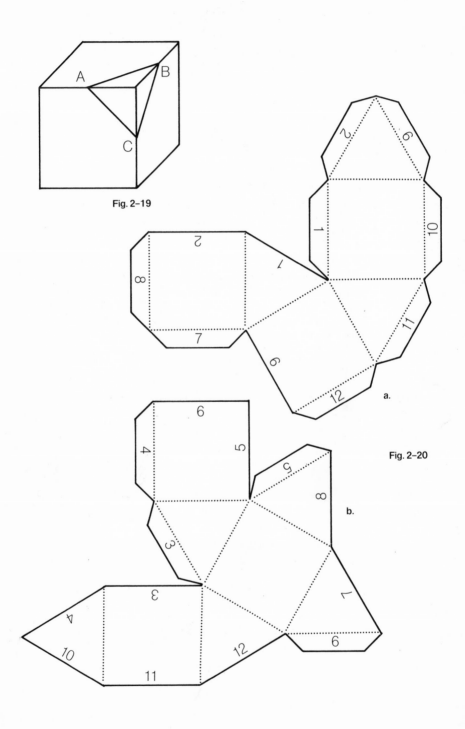

Fig. 2–19

Fig. 2–20

a.

b.

where the string you are using should be wrapped twice around the string already holding two straws together at that vertex.

A Cuboctahedron

Another space figure that starts with a cube is the cuboctahedron. It is the figure that results when eight congruent pyramids are removed, one from each vertex of the cube. Fig. 2–19 shows one of these pyramids. The midpoints of their respective edges are A, B and C. The surface of the cuboctahedron is composed of six squares and eight equilateral triangles, as you can check. You can construct a cuboctahedron by following the patterns in Fig. 2–20 and pasting matching numbers of edges and tabs together. Very stiff paper or very light cardboard will give best results. Edges 2 inches in length are suggested.

CHAPTER III
Taking Cubes Apart

In geometry the term "dissection" means the cutting apart of geometric figures. The figures can be two-dimensional or three-dimensional. Let us see what results when cubes are cut apart in various ways.

Dissecting a Cube into Two Congruent Solids

A cube can be dissected into two congruent solids as indicated in Fig. 3–1. Although three methods are shown, they are basically the same.

A cube can also be dissected into two congruent solids as indicated in Fig. 3–2. Each of the solids is composed of four of the eight minor cubes that constituted the original cube. If two halves are slid together, the original cube re-emerges.

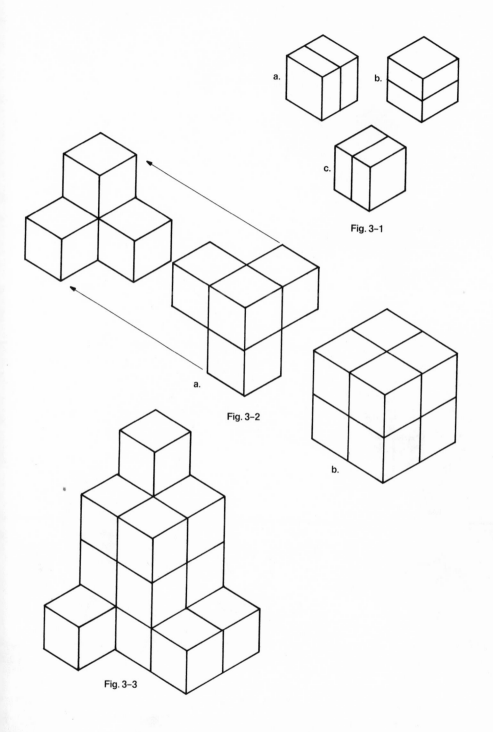

a.

b.

c.

Fig. 3-1

a.

Fig. 3-2

b.

Fig. 3-3

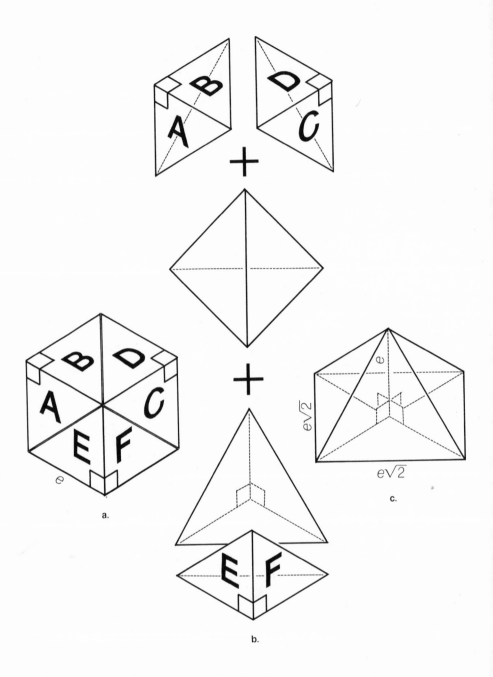

a.

b.

c.

Fig. 3-4

Dissecting a Cube into Four Congruent Solids

The figure shown in Fig. 3–3 contains sixteen smaller units. If four of these sets of sixteen are placed together we can make a cube $4 \times 4 \times 4$ composed of 64 cubic units.

Dissecting a Cube into One Regular Tetrahedron and Four Congruent Pyramids

The drawing in Fig. 3–4a represents the cutting of a cube by planes that pass through selected sets of three vertices. The result of such dissection reveals four congruent pyramids plus one regular tetrahedron (Fig. 3–4b). We can find the volume of the tetrahedron by subtracting from the volume of the cube that of the four congruent pyramids.

The distinctive feature of these pyramids is that in each case three of the six edges are mutually perpendicular. This means that each of three edges is perpendicular to the other two. If the four pyramids are rearranged as in Fig. 3-4c, a square pyramid results. The length of the base is $e\sqrt{2}$. The altitude (height of the pyramid) is of length e. The volume of the pyramid can be found through use of this formula: 1/3 area of base × height. This yields: $1/3 \times 2e^2 \times e = 2/3\,e^3$. If we subtract this from the volume of the cube, e^3, we get the volume of the regular tetrahedron. Its volume must be $1/3\,e^3$.

There is another way to find the volume of the tetrahedron (Fig. 3–5). It has for its edge the value $e\sqrt{2}$.

$$\mathbf{AB} = e\sqrt{2}$$

$$\mathbf{BD} = \frac{e\sqrt{2}}{2}$$

$\mathbf{AD}$ and $\mathbf{CD} = \dfrac{e\sqrt{6}}{2}$ (since $\mathbf{ABD}$ and $\mathbf{CDE}$ are right triangles).

$DF = 1/3$ CD, since F is the point of concurrency of the medians of the base. $DF = \dfrac{e\sqrt{6}}{6}$

$$h^2 = \frac{6e^2}{4} - \frac{6e^2}{36}$$

$$= \frac{54e^2 - 6e^2}{36} = \frac{48e^2}{36}$$

$$h = \sqrt{\frac{12e^2}{9}} = \frac{2e\sqrt{3}}{3}$$

Volume of a pyramid $= \dfrac{\text{area of base} \times \text{height}}{3}$

Area of an equilateral triangle $= \dfrac{\text{side}^2\sqrt{3}}{4}$

Volume of a regular tetrahedron

$$= \frac{1}{3} \times \frac{(e\sqrt{2})^2\sqrt{3}}{4} \times \frac{2e\sqrt{3}}{3}$$

$$= \frac{1}{3} \times \frac{2e^2\sqrt{3}}{4} \times \frac{2e\sqrt{3}}{3}$$

$$= \frac{4e^3 \times 3}{36}$$

$$= \frac{1}{3}e^3$$

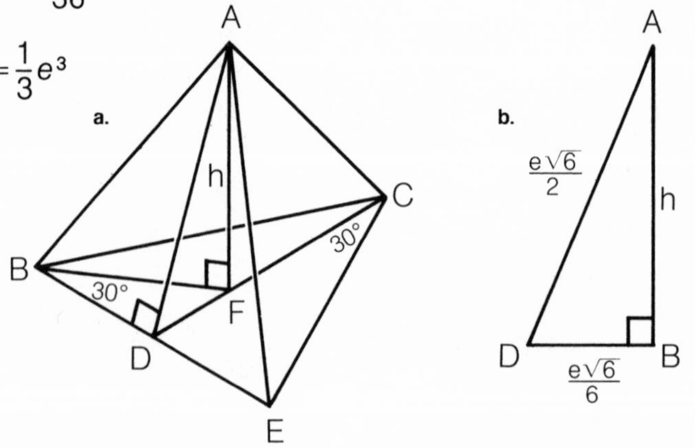

Fig. 3-5

This result means that the regular tetrahedron occupies just one-third of the cube in which it is inscribed. Since the four congruent pyramids occupy the other two thirds of the cube, the regular tetrahedron is equal in volume to two of the four pyramids. So . . . if the cube held three gallons of water, one gallon would fill the regular tetrahedron, another gallon would fill two of the pyramids, and the other gallon would fill the other two pyramids.

The material just discussed enables us to go on to dissect a cube into two congruent parts in an interesting manner. The regular tetrahedron can be dissected into two congruent solids as indicated in Fig. 3–6a. This can be accomplished by passing a plane through points **A**, **B**, **C** and **D**, midpoints of the four edges. The resulting quadrilateral **ABCD** is always a square. The two solids resting on the common base **ABCD** are rotated 90 degrees from each other. The dimensions of each edge of the half-tetrahedron have been indicated.

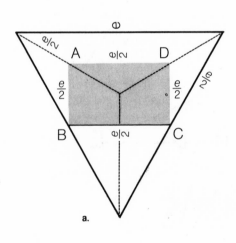

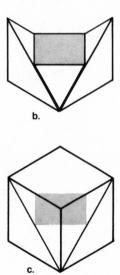

Fig. 3–6

Figure 3–6b shows half of the original cube. It is composed of two of the triangular pyramids and half of the regular tetrahedron. If a solid identical to the first one is turned upside down, then rotated 90 degrees, it will fit to form the rest of the cube (Fig. 3–6c).

Dissecting a Cube into Four Congruent Hexahedrons

If vertices **A**, **B**, **C** and **D** of any cube are all connected to one another, a regular tetrahedron will be formed. Each of its six edges will be $e\sqrt{2}$ units in length (Fig. 3–7a). If the center

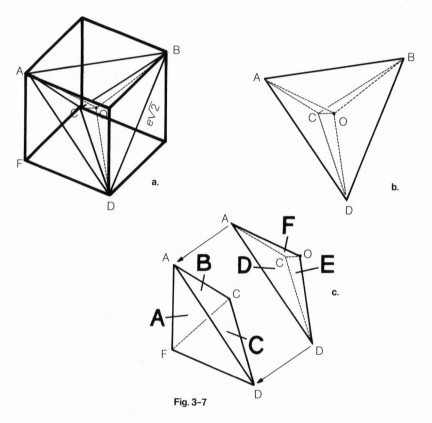

Fig. 3–7

of any regular tetrahedron is joined to its four vertices, four congruent pyramids will be formed around that center (Fig. 3–7b). This means that solid **AFDCO** in Fig. 3–7a is ¹/₄ of the original cube. Hence any cube can be dissected into four congruent hexahedrons. Three of the six faces of these hexahedrons will be congruent right triangles—A,B,C (Fig. 3–7c). The other three will be congruent isosceles triangles—D,E,F (Fig. 3–7c).

The lengths of **AF**, **FC** and **DF** will be: e
The lengths of **AD**, **AC** and **CD** will be: $e\sqrt{2}$

The lengths of **AO**, **CO** and **DO** will be $\dfrac{e\sqrt{6}}{4}$

Suggestions on the calculations involved in reaching this value are in Fig. 3–7. The 30°–60°–90° relations play an important part in many of these calculations.

Dissecting a Cube into Smaller Cubes

It is possible to dissect a cube into subcubes in a number of ways. Three planes, drawn as in Fig. 3–8a, will cut a cube into eight congruent subcubes. Two of these planes are vertical, at right angles to each other. The other is horizontal. Six planes, drawn as in Fig. 3–8b, will cut a cube into 27 congruent subcubes. Here four planes are vertical; two are horizontal.

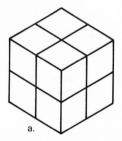 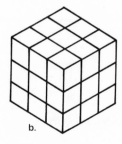 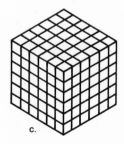

Fig. 3–8

In the first example eight subcubes have been formed. In the second example 27 congruent subcubes have been formed. In general, if each edge of a cube is divided into n equal segments, the totality of subcubes is n^3. The number of planes necessary to produce this dissection will be $3(n-1)$. *For example:* if each edge of the cube in Fig. 3–8c is divided into six equal segments, there will be 216 congruent subcubes. It will take 15 planes to produce this number of subcubes. "Subcube" refers to a cube whose length is e/n.

There are, of course, many cubes within the original whose lengths are multiples of the lengths of the subcubes referred to. What formula will predict the totality of subcubes of *all* types? (We know, but we're not going to tell.)

There are many rectangular solids within the original cube. What formula will predict the total number of solids?

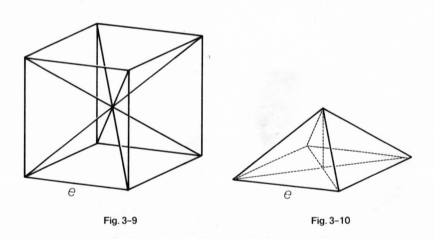

Fig. 3–9   Fig. 3–10

Dissecting a Cube into Pyramids

It is possible to separate a cube into six congruent pyramids (Fig. 3–9). This can be done by constructing the four

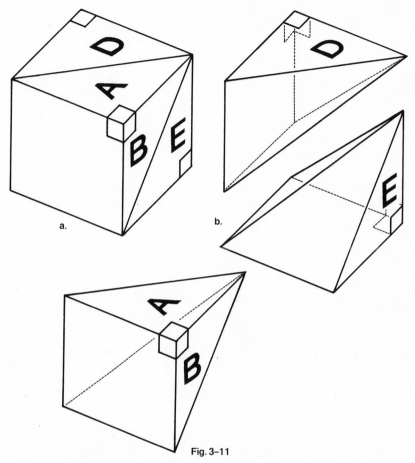

Fig. 3–11

interior diagonals of the cube. Since each of these six pyramids can be divided into four smaller congruent pyramids (Fig. 3–10), the original cube can be dissected into 24 congruent pyramids. Each will have a volume of $e^3/24$.

It is also possible to dissect a cube into three congruent pyramids as in Fig. 3–11a and b. The eight edges of each of the pyramids are composed of the following types: there are five edges whose length is that of the original cube; there are two whose lengths are $e\sqrt{2}$; there is one whose length is that of the interior diagonal of the cube. Its value is $e\sqrt{3}$.

General Principles of Dissection

A more generalized examination of the problem of cube dissection reveals the following:

1. The original cube, intact and untouched, represents the dissection of the cube into one part—a trivial solution.

2. In *two* dimensions, any straight line that passes through the center of a square will dissect it into *two* congruent regions (Fig. 3–12a). As is often the case in examining relations in the cube, the square supplies clues. In *three* dimensions, any plane passed through the center of the cube will divide it into two congruent solids. Several cases are illustrated in Fig. 3–12b–e.

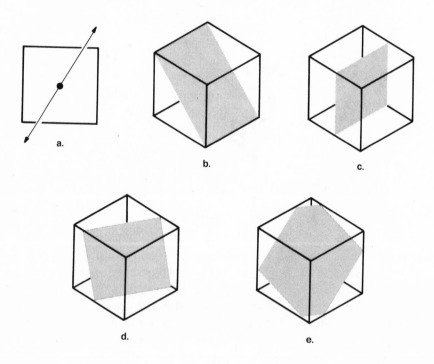

Fig. 3–12

3. Planes passed parallel to a face of a cube at equal intervals (Fig. 3–13) will separate it into three, four, five and so on to n congruent parts. Some of these dissections can, of course, be accomplished in other ways. We have already examined in the previous section the case where the cube was dissected into three congruent pyramids.

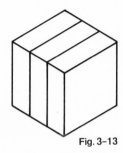

Fig. 3–13

4. Dissection into four congruent parts offers a variety of solutions in addition to the one mentioned above. Let **AB** (Fig. 3–14a) join the centers of opposite faces of a cube. In *two* dimensions, any pair of perpendicular lines that pass through the center of a square will separate the square into four congruent regions (Fig. 3–14b). If the two perpendicular planes X and Y intersect along the axis **AB** (Fig. 3–14c), the intersection of these planes with the cube will result in four congruent solids.

Since the perpendicular planes can rotate about **AB** as axis, it is evident that there are many possible dissections. Several of these are illustrated in Fig. 3–14d–f.

We can use these illustrations to supply clues to further dissections. Suppose that planes were to be passed parallel to each of the bases of the cubes shown in Fig. 3–14d–f. If these planes were to divide the cubes vertically into n equal parallel regions, the entire cube would then be divided into 4n congruent parts. One of the many ways of dividing a cube into 24 congruent parts is shown in Fig. 3–14g.

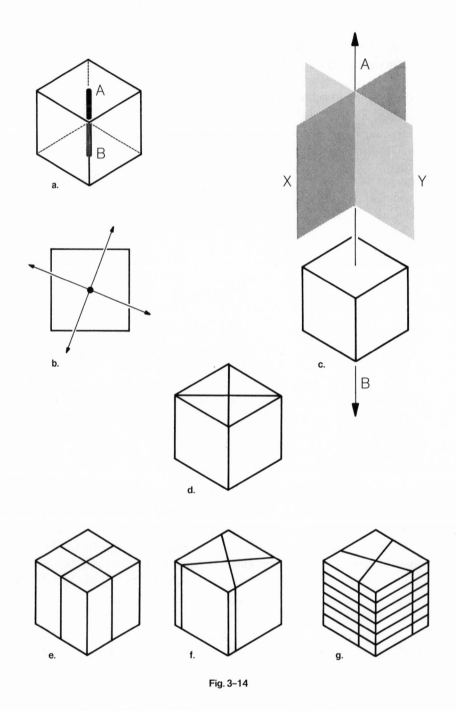

Fig. 3–14

Exposing the Interior Surface of a Cube

Suppose we begin with a cube one inch on a side. It, like all cubes, has six exterior faces (Fig. 3–15a). To cut this cube into smaller cubes, at least three cuts, two vertical and one horizontal (Fig. 3–15b), are necessary. The interior surfaces exposed will contain six square inches. Don't forget that each cut exposes two interior faces (Fig. 3–15c).

If each face is cut twice (Fig. 3–15d), the interior surface exposed will contain 12 square inches.

If each face is cut three times (Fig. 3–15e), the interior surface exposed will contain 18 square inches. We can predict the total surface exposed from the table in Fig. 3–16.

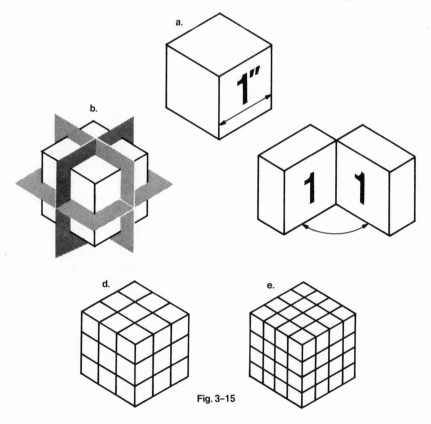

Fig. 3–15

No. of cuts per face	0	1	2	3	n
Interior surface exposed	0	6 sq. in.	12 sq. in.	18 sq. in.	6n sq. in.

Fig. 3–16

As the number of cuts per face increases, the interior surface exposed increases. If we could keep this up long enough, we could expose a surface as large as we wanted. We should be able to expose a surface as large as that of the world!

Examining the Exterior Surfaces of a Cube

The exterior surface of a cube that is e units on a side is $6e^2$ square units (Fig. 3–17a). If it is cut once vertically (Fig. 3–17b), the exposed surface is now $8e^2$ square units. If it is cut again vertically, in a direction perpendicular to the original vertical, the exterior surface will now be $10e^2$ square units (Fig. 3–17c). A third cut horizontally (Fig. 3–17d) will raise the exposed surfaces to $12e^2$ square units. In each case, the cut has been made midway on an edge. This is not really necessary but will make the work in this section simpler. Note that there are two basic vertical sections, perpendicular to each other, and one horizontal section.

Suppose that we follow the scheme presented above, cutting each face first once, then twice, then three times and so on. Figure 3–18 can be used to record the statistics for the maneuvers. Thus, a cube 10 inches on a side (Fig. 3–19), with an original exterior surface of 600 square inches, when cut nine times on a face will produce an exterior surface of $6(9+1) \times 100$, or 6,000 square inches! . . . This is why we grind coffee beans to make better coffee. We expose more surface this way.

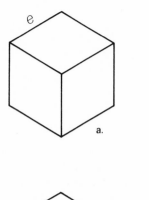 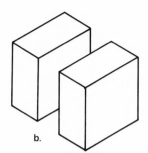

a. b.

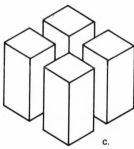 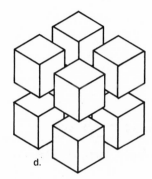

c. d.

Fig. 3–17

No. of cuts per face	0	1	2	3	4	5	n
Exterior surface exposed	$6e^2$	$12e^2$	$18e^2$	$24e^2$	$30e^2$	$36e^2$	$6(n+1)e^2$

Fig. 3–18

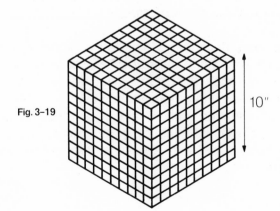

Fig. 3–19

10″

CHAPTER IV
Cross Sections of a Cube

You can give your imagination quite a workout by thinking of ways of cutting up cubes. Think of a cube made of wood. Imagine sawing through it at various angles. Each angle of cut will produce a cross section. These cross sections would be of various types. In Fig. 4–1a the cross section is a square, in Fig. 4–1b it is a rectangle and in Fig. 4–1c it is a pentagon.

Now the plot thickens. Consider a plane surface intersecting a cube. Since the cube has six faces, the greatest number of faces the plane can intersect is six. The whole list of possibilities consists of (1) intersection with no faces, (2) intersection with 1 face, (3) intersection with 2 faces, etc., up to (7) intersection with 6 faces.

In this chapter, we shall examine each of these cases more closely.

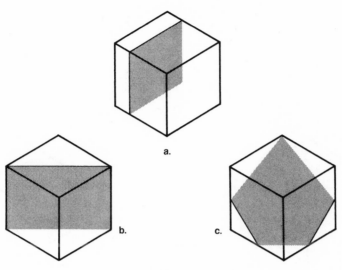

Fig. 4–1

Intersection of a Plane with No Faces

In this case (Fig. 4–2a), there are no intersections whatever; there can be no points in common. If the plane is tangent to a corner of the cube (Fig. 4–2b), there is one point common to the plane and the surface of the cube. The plane has freedom to rotate in many directions. If the cube occupies $1/8$ of three-dimensional space (after all, eight identical cubes can be piled around a point in space), the plane can rotate within $7/8$ of three-dimensional space.

If the plane is tangent to an edge (Fig. 4–2c), the intersection will be a line segment. Here again the plane has freedom of rotation. This freedom of rotation is within $3/4$ of three-dimensional space.

Intersection of a Plane with One Face

If the rotation of the plane is such that it includes, besides a corner point and an edge, a *face* of the cube, the cross sec-

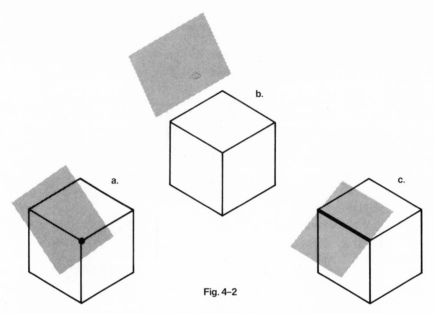

Fig. 4-2

tion will be a square (Fig. 4–3). The only possible way a plane can intersect a single face is to coincide with it. The face becomes part of the plane.

Intersection of a Plane with Two Faces

At this time it is well to recall a basic theorem of solid geometry: If a plane intersects two parallel planes, the lines of intersection will always be parallel (Fig. 4–4a). Since the surfaces of the cube are parts of three pairs of parallel planes, this theorem will come in handy in the rest of this discussion.

If a plane is to intersect two faces of the cube, two possible cases arise:

Case 1. Intersection with A and B, adjoining surfaces (Fig. 4–4b). Intersection with A and B will involve intersection with at least one extra face.

Case 2. Intersection with A and C, parallel surfaces (Fig. 4–4c). Intersection with A and C will involve at least two extra faces.

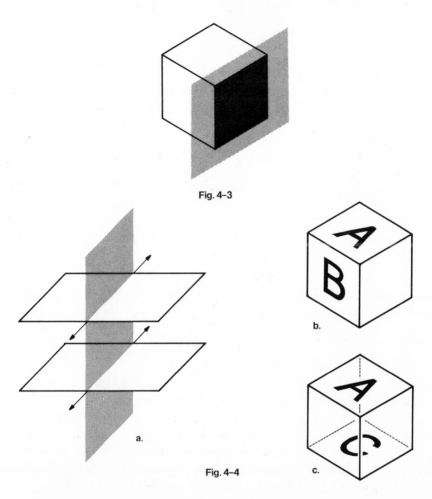

Fig. 4–3

b.

a.

Fig. 4–4

c.

Intersection with either A and B or A and C will always involve intersection with at least one other face. Thus, intersections that involve *exactly* two faces of the cube cannot
exist. There is one exception. This occurs when a plane is
passed through two diagonally opposite edges. This produces a rectangular cross section (see Fig. 4–1b).

This can, of course, be argued, since edges occur when
faces intersect each other.

43

Intersection of a Plane with Three Faces

Intersections with three faces of a cube are of two types.

Case 1. The first involves three faces with a common intersection, such as faces A, B and C in Fig. 4–5a. Any plane that intersects A, B and C will generate a triangle. Such triangles will be of three types: scalene (three unequal sides), isosceles (two equal sides) or equilateral (three equal sides).

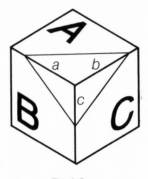

Fig. 4–5a

In order to generate a scalene triangle it will be sufficient if lengths *a, b* and *c* are unequal. Once values of *a, b* and *c* have been selected, a plane can be passed through the three points. A scalene triangle will then be generated. Such triangles will always contain three acute angles. None of the angles can ever be right or obtuse. Every plane passed through the cube parallel to the plane of this triangle will produce triangles similar to the original triangle. The whole process is similar to what occurs when cheese is sliced in an automatic slicer. The planes may intersect *only* adjoining surfaces such as A, B and C. If other surfaces are met, the polygons will no longer be triangles.

If two of the three values *a, b* and *c* are equal, the triangles generated will be isosceles. If all three values are alike, equilateral triangles will be formed. If *a, b* and *c* are taken as the original edges of the cube, the equilateral triangle formed will be the largest triangle possible (Fig. 4–5b). If the edge of the original cube is taken as e, the area of such an equilateral triangle will be: $\dfrac{e^2\sqrt{3}}{2} = .866e^2$. Eight such equilateral triangles are possible in each cube.

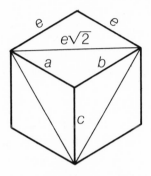

Fig. 4–5b

Case 2. The second type of intersection with three faces involves three faces that have no points in common, such as A, B and C in Fig. 4–6. In these cases, two of the faces, such as A and C, must be parallel. Any plane that in-

Fig. 4–6

tersects A, B and C will have to meet D, the face opposite B, or face F. The cross section will be a quadrilateral; it cannot be a triangle. Obviously, this case does not produce an intersection with *exactly* three faces.

Intersection of a Plane with Four Faces

Intersections with four faces of a cube are basically of two types: In type 1, A, B, C and D (the faces that the plane intersects) are related so that A is parallel to C and B is parallel to D (Fig. 4–7a). In type 2, A is parallel to C, but B intersects D (Fig. 4–7b).

Case 1. Any plane that intersects A, B, C and D will have a parallelogram as a cross section. This is a result of the principle that the intersection of parallel planes with a third plane always results in parallel lines.

If $WX = WZ$ (Fig. 4–7c), the parallelogram will be a rhombus. The shorter diagonal of such a rhombus (XZ in Fig. 4–7c) will be of length $e\sqrt{2}$.

When a plane is passed through W, Y, M and M', midpoints of their respective edges (Fig. 4–7d), the rhombus will be of maximum area. Diagonal WY of this rhombus has a value of $e\sqrt{3}$, and diagonal MM' is $e\sqrt{2}$.

The area of a rhombus can be found by taking half the product of the diagonals. Thus the area here will be:

$$\frac{e^2 \times \sqrt{3} \times \sqrt{2}}{2} = 1.225e^2.$$ There are twelve of these maximum-area rhombuses in every cube. We have seen that the shorter diagonal of such rhombuses is the segment that joins the midpoints of opposite edges of the cube. There are six such segments and two rhombuses per segment.

Under special circumstances the rhombus will be a square. This will occur when planes are passed parallel to any of the six squares that bound the cube (Fig. 4–7e).

Under other circumstances the parallelograms normally

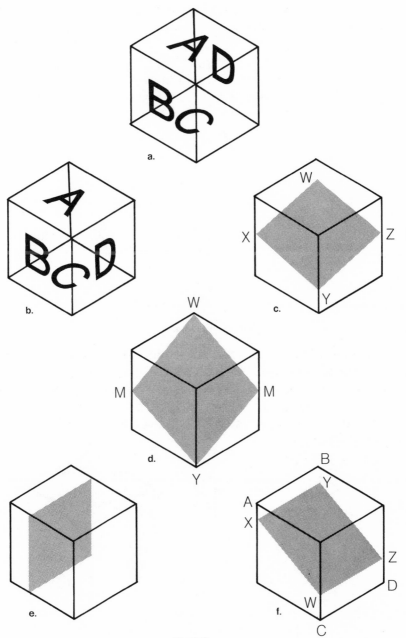

Fig. 4–7

formed in type 1 turn out to be rectangles (Fig. 4–7f). If **XY** is parallel to **AB**, **WXYZ** will be a rectangle. **AX** need not equal **CW**.

Case 2. Fig. 4–7b offers interesting possibilities for the generation of squares different from those that occur in type 1. **ABCD** (Fig. 4–8a) is one of the surfaces of a cube. It is

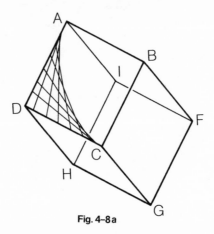

Fig. 4–8a

apparent that any of the segments shown drawn on **ABCD** has a length equal to the side of the cube. If a plane is passed through any one of these segments, parallel to an edge of the cube (**AI, BF, CG,** or **DH**), a whole series of square cross-sections will be formed (Fig. 4–8b). This ma-

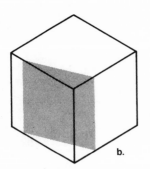
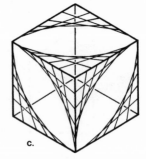

Fig. 4–8

neuver can be carried out at any of the four corners of a face. Consequently there are 12 sets of the "whirling" square cross sections. One set of four is vertical. A second set is horizontal, and a third set is also horizontal—but oriented 90 degrees from the first horizontal set (Fig. 4–8c).

Figure 4–9a illustrates the idea of a plane parallel to a line. Every plane at the left is parallel to line *l* *except* the one on which line *l* lies. It is understood that the planes can be extended through space.

If planes are passed through the cube parallel to any one of the edges, sets of rectangles will be generated (Fig. 4–9b). The rectangle whose length is that of the diagonal of one of the faces is of particular interest. If the edge of the cube is e, the diagonal has a value of $e\sqrt{2}$. The area of the rectangle is $e^2\sqrt{2}$, about $1.414e^2$ (Fig. 4–9c).

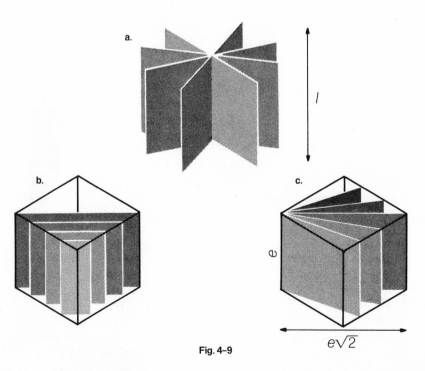

Fig. 4–9

$e\sqrt{2}$

Case 2 (Fig. 4–7b) offers other possibilities for discovery. Remember that surfaces A and C are parallel; surfaces B and D intersect. If a plane is to intersect surfaces A, B, C and D, the cross section formed will have to have at least two edges parallel. After all, A is parallel to C, and a plane that intersects these squares will leave traces of parallel segments. Hence the most common cross section will be a trapezoid (Fig. 4–10a). Under special circumstances the

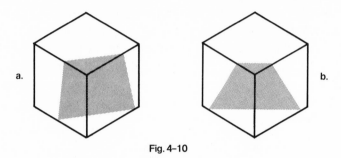

a.   b.

Fig. 4–10

trapezoid will be isosceles. A little reflection will show that this will occur when the plane is passed through the cube parallel to the diagonal of a face (Fig. 4–10b). Sometimes the upper base of the trapezoid is smaller than the lower one. Sometimes the situation is reversed. Sometimes the trapezoid is transformed into a rectangle. Sometimes this rectangle is a square. In *any* case, the polygon formed will have at *least* two sides parallel.

Intersection of a Plane with Five Faces

Intersections with five faces of a cube will produce pentagons. These pentagons will be of a special type. It is impossible to select five of the six bounding surfaces of a cube without selecting two pairs of parallel surfaces among the five. Any plane that intersects these five surfaces must, then, form a pentagon in which four of these five edges are parallel by pairs. This is a result of the theorem on the intersection of parallel planes by a third. The plane geometry principle of such configurations is illustrated in Fig. 4–11a. The three-dimensional attribute is shown in Fig. 4–11b.

The cross section of a cube will be a pentagon if, and only if, a plane passes through one of the corners of the original cube. Such a plane must, of course, intersect five surfaces of the cube.

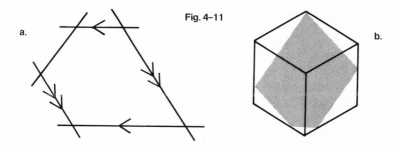

Fig. 4–11

a.

b.

Intersection of a Plane with Six Faces

Intersections with six faces of a cube will result in hexagons. Such hexagons will always have opposite sides parallel by pairs (again as a result of the parallel-plane theorem). Howard Eves of the University of Maine calls these examples of par-polygons. According to his definition, such polygons always have an even number of sides, parallel by pairs. A parallelogram is, for example, also a par-polygon. Fig. 4–12a illustrates a par-hexagon. This is a typical intersection formed when a plane meets six faces of a cube. Under special circumstances the hexagon formed may also be equilateral. This makes the hexagon *regular,* both equilateral and equiangular (see Fig. 2–7, page 12).

A regular hexagon is formed when a plane is the perpendicular bisector of one of the four interior diagonals of the cube. Thus, there are four such regular hexagons. Another way of forming these regular hexagons is by joining appro-

51

priate midpoints of the edges of a cube. This principle is illustrated in Fig. 4–12b. The area of this basic regular hexagon can be compared with some of the other areas already discussed. Side **AB** is of length $\frac{e\sqrt{2}}{2}$. The area of the regular hexagon can be found through the use of the formula for the area of an equilateral triangle. Six congruent equilateral triangles converging at a point form a regular hexagon (Fig. 4–12c). Since the area of an equilateral triangle can be found through the use of the formula $\frac{side^2\sqrt{3}}{4}$, the area of a regular hexagon will be $\frac{6\times side^2\sqrt{3}}{4}$. Since each side is of length $\frac{e\sqrt{2}}{2}$, the area of the regular hexagon will be $\frac{3}{4}e^2\sqrt{3}=1.299e^2$.

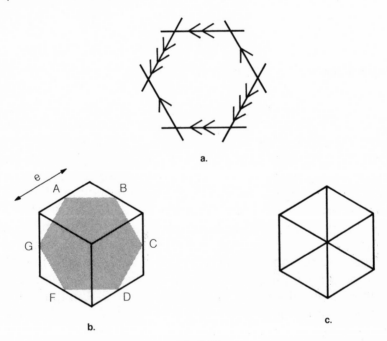

a.

b.

c.

Fig. 4–12

Typical Cross Sections of a Cube

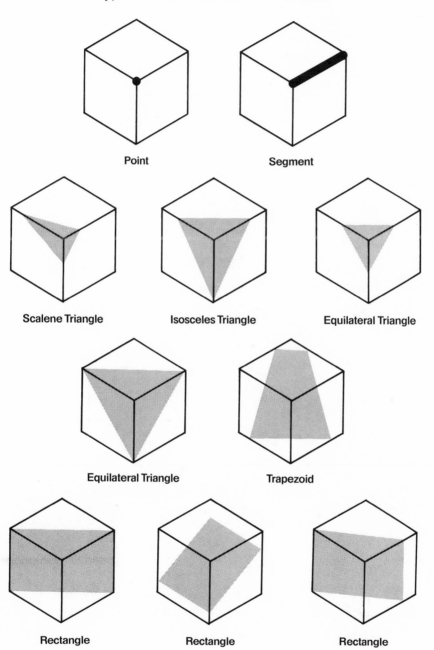

Point

Segment

Scalene Triangle

Isosceles Triangle

Equilateral Triangle

Equilateral Triangle

Trapezoid

Rectangle

Rectangle

Rectangle

Typical Cross Sections of a Cube

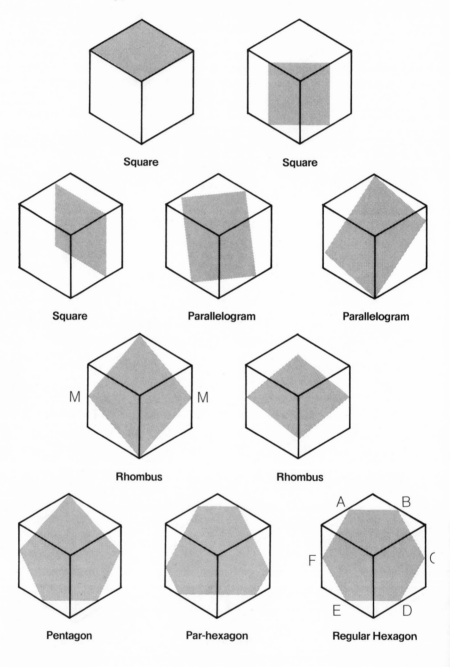

Square

Square

Square

Parallelogram

Parallelogram

Rhombus

Rhombus

Pentagon

Par-hexagon

Regular Hexagon

Summary

At this time, a summary of our findings with regard to areas may be worthy of attention.

The triangle with maximum area is the equilateral triangle with side $e\sqrt{2}$. The value of its area is: $.866e^2$

The rectangle with maximum area has dimensions e and $e\sqrt{2}$. The value of its area is: $1.414e^2$

The square with maximum (and minimum) area has a length of e. The value of its area is: $1.000e^2$

The rhombus (not a square) with maximum area has a side of $\dfrac{e\sqrt{5}}{2}$. The value of its area is: $1.225e^2$

The hexagon with maximum area is regular. The length of its side is $\dfrac{e\sqrt{2}}{2}$. The value of its area is: $1.299e^2$

It looks as though the rectangle with a length that of the diagonal of a face of the cube and a width that of the edge of the cube has the largest area of any of these polygons.

A summary of our findings with regard to cross sections of the cube which are regular polygons shows the following:

1. There is an infinite number of cross sections that are equilateral triangles. They can be generated by passing planes through the cube perpendicular to one of the four interior diagonals of the cube. Such planes may intersect only three surfaces of the cube.

2. There is but one size square that can be a cross section. There is an infinite number of such squares.

3. A regular pentagon cannot possibly be a cross section of a cube. The mechanics of the regular pentagon, as indicated by Fig. 4–13a, show no possibility of the occurrence of parallel edges. Since every pentagonal cross section of a cube must involve two pairs of parallel edges, no pentagonal cross section of a cube can be regular.

4. There is but one basic regular hexagon that can be a cross section of a given cube. There are, however, four such hexagons possible in any one cube. There is an infi-

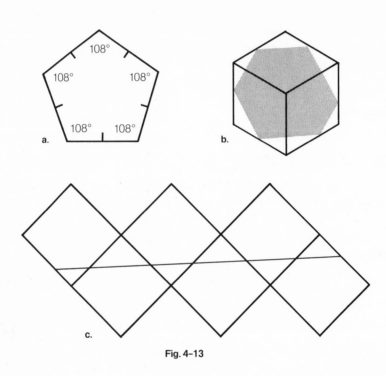

Fig. 4–13

nite number of *par-hexagons* possible. Every plane that intersects the six faces of a cube is bound to generate such a polygon. Such a par-hexagon is shown on the surface of the cube in Fig. 4–13b and c. The traces of this polygon have been drawn on the flattened surface of the cube for simplicity.

CHAPTER V
The Geometry of the Cube

Drawing a Cube

The cube is a three-dimensional figure. One usually discusses its geometry in terms of three dimensions. Even then, it is often necessary to draw a picture of a cube. This must be done on a two-dimensional surface—a piece of paper, for example. Let us begin this chapter, then, by considering the problem of drawing the cube—that is, of representing this three-dimensional shape on a two-dimensional surface.

There are many ways of drawing a representation of the cube. Each one has its advantages. One tries to pick the method that emphasizes the features of the cube which are most important to the message he wants to convey.

Consider once more the statistics of the cube. It has twelve equal edges. There are six congruent faces, which are squares. Considering just the right angles involved in the six faces, there are twenty-four. The cube has eight vertices symmetrically placed with respect to its center. At each vertex there is an edge perpendicular to two converging edges.

Let us analyze each of the seven representations in Fig. 5–1a–g.

a. This is the drawing commonly used in isometric projection. Its main advantage is that distortions of length, width and height are balanced. One disadvantage is that the front edge blocks the diagonal of the base. In addition, none of the angles observed is a right angle.

b. Here two of the faces actually appear as squares. Eight angles presented are really right angles. There is some distortion. However, the twelve edges may be drawn equal.

c. Drawing c, to be discussed more thoroughly on page 103, is a type of projection called a "rabbatment." We are pretending that the front face of the cube is transparent. As we look through the front face we see the rest of the cube in perspective. This view is excellent when we are trying to get an overall picture of all the components of the cube. There is, however, a great deal of distortion.

d. This view of a cube is drawn in one-point perspective. The four receding edges meet at O, the vanishing point. This type of representation presents the cube somewhat as the eye would actually see it. Eight angles are actually right angles. There is, however, distortion of the sides.

e. Here two-point perspective is used. This is as the eye would actually see a cube oriented with one of the vertical edges directly in front of the point of vision. We can arrange to see more or less of the upper face of the cube by raising or lowering the levels of vanishing points. None of the angles is actually a right angle.

f. Here three-point perspective is being used. This would be the view we would get of a cube if we were up in an airplane.

58

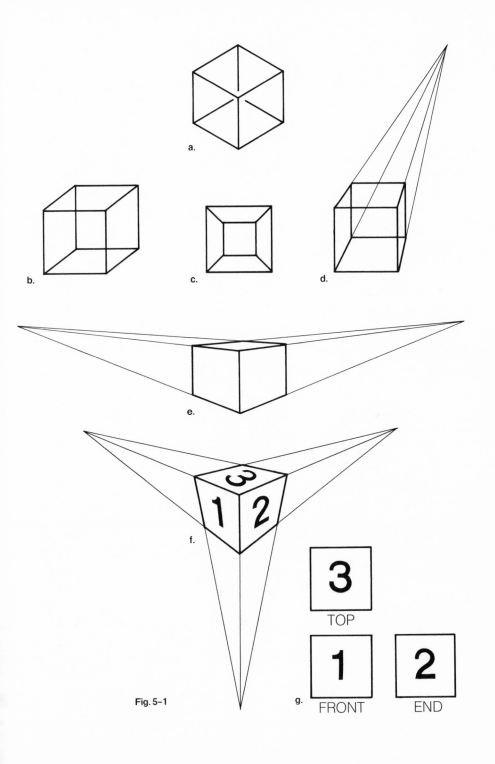

a.

b.

c.

d.

e.

f.

g.

3
TOP

1
FRONT

2
END

Fig. 5-1

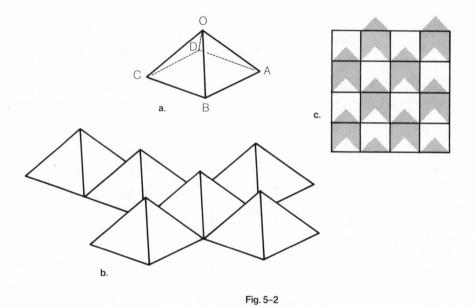

a.

b.

c.

Fig. 5-2

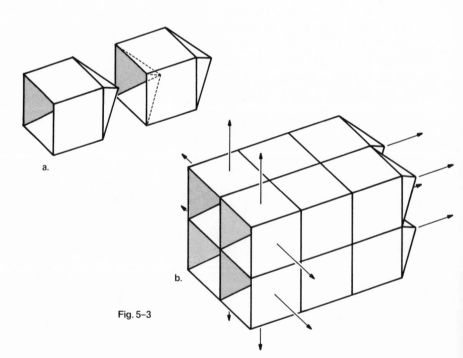

a.

b.

Fig. 5-3

g. Here the three separate views of the cube are those obtained through orthographic projection. No attempt is made to capture a third dimension. We are interested in true views of the front, top and ends of a cube. Such drawings are handy when one is trying to convey actual measurements of three-dimensional objects.

Three-dimensional Space Filling

There is a limited number of ways of filling three-dimensional space with congruent solid units. Such occurrences are termed "solid tessellations." Probably the simplest way of filling three-dimensional space is with congruent cubes. Children's blocks are a common example of this. Repetition of any rectangular solid would also result in a filling of space. If you took dominos and stacked them regularly, space would be filled.

Discussion here will be limited to those tessellations that are based upon congruent cubes.

The diagonals of a cube intersect at its center at a point equidistant from the six faces. This means that six congruent pyramids meet at the center of any cube. The volume of each of these pyramids will be $1/6$ that of the cube: $e^3/6$. The dimensions of this basic pyramid will be **AB**, **BC**, **CD**, **DA**, all with value e, or edge; **AO**, **BO**, **CO**, **DO**, all with value $\frac{e\sqrt{3}}{2}$. (Each has a value that is half that of the diagonal of the cube.) See Fig. 5–2a.

If the cube is opened as in Fig. 5–2b, it will be seen that one of the pyramids rests on each of the six faces of the original cube.

By combining cubes with the pyramids just discussed, it may be possible to fill space with shapes more imaginative than cubes. An analogy with the two-dimensional space-filling pattern of Fig. 5–2c may give some clues to three dimensions.

Case 1. Consider the cube with one of the pyramids removed from one end of the cube and built up on the opposite face (Fig. 5–3a). The volume of this new solid, which we plan to use as a basic unit for space filling, is still e^3. Since such solids nest, it would be possible to fill space as indicated in Fig. 5–3b. Other rows like those indicated could be placed above, below, to the right, to the left, to the front, to the back, etc. The resulting assembly could be spread as far as desired.

Case 2. The unit just investigated could be modified as in Fig. 5–4. Here the protruding-receding technique has

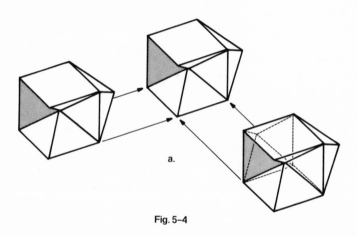

a.

Fig. 5–4

been carried out twice. The result of this maneuver enables us to "cement" rows and columns on a horizontal plane. Each protruding pyramid fills the cavity of its neighbor. Note that **BO′CO″** (Fig. 5–4c) will now be a coplanar unit—a rhombus, in fact. A similar device is used for protection around nuclear reactors. Lead blocks are made so that they interlock. There is less chance for accidental penetration by gamma rays this way. The V-edge protrudes on two adjacent edges of the original lead block and recedes on the two other edges. Walls are easily constructed with these V blocks (Fig. 5–4d).

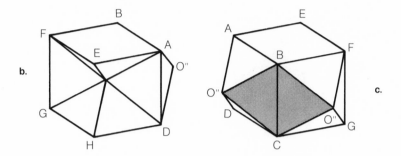

The basic unit looks, from one point of view, like the drawing in Fig. 5–4b. From another point of view, it looks like the drawing in Fig. 5–4c.

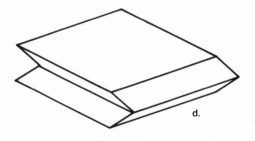

Fig. 5–4

Case 3. If the same technique is carried out on three pairs of parallel faces (Fig. 5–5a), we can "cement" the assembly in three ways—two horizontally and one vertically. The units we are now using will stack vertically. They will also stack horizontally, in two directions, h_1 and h_2 (Fig. 5–5b). These will be perpendicular to each other. In this stacking of units, three congruent rhombuses will result. These are: **ABCD**, **ADFE** and **CDFG**.

Case 4. The technique used in Case 3 need not involve protruding and receding *pyramids.* If *any* form is exca-

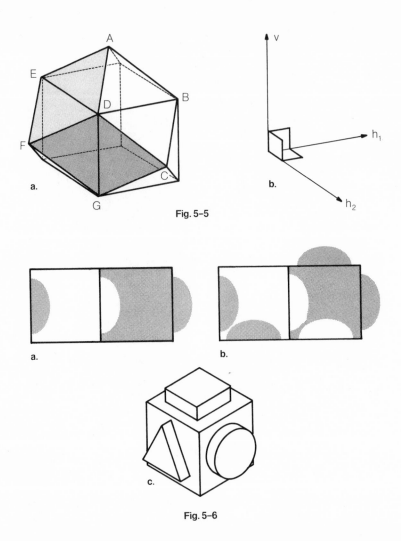

Fig. 5-5

Fig. 5-6

vated from one face of a cube and replaced at the opposite face, similar stacking possibilities result. Examine the two-dimensional counterparts in Figs. 5–6a and b for clues to this type of space filling. One three-dimensional example is shown in Fig. 5–6c. Note that the added surfaces are not necessarily congruent to each other.

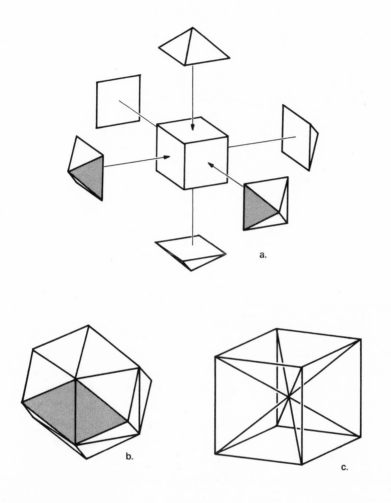

Fig. 5–7

Case 5. If one of the pyramids is built up on each of the faces of a cube, the solid that results has a volume of $2e^3$ (Fig. 5–7a). The lateral faces of one of the pyramids are always coplanar with the adjacent faces of other pyramids. The result is a solid of 12 faces, a rhombic dodecahedron. Its 12 faces are all congruent rhombuses (Fig. 5–7b).

If e is the edge of the cube, the edge of each of the rhombuses has the value of $\frac{e\sqrt{3}}{2}$. This is the value of half of the diagonal of the cube.

The spatial unit just discussed is an example of what is sometimes termed an "extroverted regular solid" or a "polyhedron." It is just as though the cube had been turned inside out, starting at its original center. The eight dots in Fig. 5–7b represent the vertices of the original cube.

In a similar manner, we may speak of an introverted cube. Here we have a nonsolid solid consisting of just the framework of the cube including the four interior diagonals. This configuration is pictured in Fig. 5–7c. It is analogous to a hollowed-out cube. It has nine vertices, 20 edges, and no volume.

Regular Solids and Duality

The cube is one of five solids that are called the regular polyhedrons. Each of these solids has congruent regular polygons for faces. (A regular polygon has congruent edges and congruent angles.) Every solid angle in such regular polyhedrons is congruent to every other. (A solid angle results when two or more planes intersect.) The cube is, then, a regular polyhedron because:

1. Its six faces are congruent squares.
2. At each of its eight vertices three squares come together at a point.

If the center of each of the six faces of a cube is connected to the center of all the other faces (Fig. 5–8), a regular octahedron will emerge. Each of its eight faces will be an equilateral triangle congruent to each of the others. The solid angle at each of the vertices will be composed of four 60-degree angles. The edge of the regular octahedron has

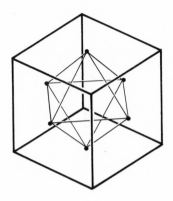

Fig. 5–8

the value of $\dfrac{e\sqrt{2}}{2}$. If the vital statistics of the cube are examined with reference to those of the regular octahedron, the same numbers occur. They are, however, used in a different capacity; this is an example of *duality*. Thus, the regular octahedron is said to be the dual of the cube.

	Cube	Octahedron
Number of vertices	8	6
Number of faces	6	8
Number of edges	12	12

The regular polyhedrons are important in such studies as crystallography. In ancient times they were of great interest in matters of mythology and religion.

If four of the eight vertices of a cube are properly selected (**A,C,H,F**), a regular tetrahedron emerges (Fig. 5–9a). If the other four vertices (**B,D,G,E**) are joined, another regular tetrahedron is bounded (Fig. 5–9b). Where these two tetrahedrons intersect, a regular *octahedron* is enclosed (Fig. 5–9c). Thus, in one configuration, we encounter three out of the five possible regular solids.

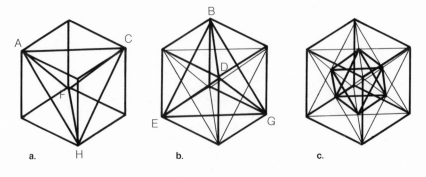

Fig. 5-9

Skewed Regular Polygons

Skewed regular polygons, commonly called "Petrie" polygons, must be both equilateral and equiangular. "Skewed" here refers to the fact that in skewed figures not all the elements are coplanar.

Present in the configurations formed by the twelve edges of a cube are several Petrie polygons. Polygon **ABCDEF-A** (Fig. 5–10a) is a skewed regular hexagon. It is, obviously, equilateral. It is equiangular because its angles are all 90

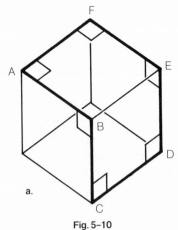

Fig. 5-10

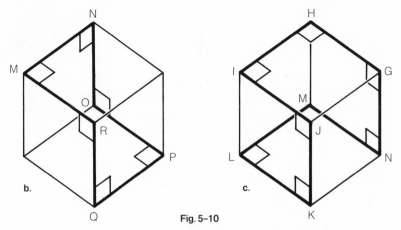

Fig. 5–10

degrees. In some cases the plane of the 90 degrees is vertical. In other cases the planes are horizontal. Polygon **MNOPQR–M** (Fig. 5–10b) is also a skewed regular hexagon. Polygon **GHIJKLMN–G** (Fig. 5–10c) is a skewed regular octagon.

There are other Petrie polygons formed by diagonals of the faces of a cube. Polygon **ABCD–A** in Fig. 5–10d is a skewed regular quadrilateral. Its vertex angles each contain 60 degrees. Each of its four sides has the value $e\sqrt{2}$ units.

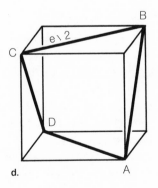

Fig. 5–10

Pohlke's Theorem

A theorem discovered in 1858 by K. W. Pohlke, the Polish mathematician, and published in 1860 without proof, states the following: Select a point **A** (Fig. 5–11a). Draw three segments from this point. Complete parallelograms as shown. The resulting figure may be considered as a possible view of a cube. The view is normally oblique, or slanting. Other possible views appear in Fig. 5–11b and c.

Here are some special cases suggested by Pohlke's Theorem.

In Fig. 5–11d the eye is directly above a prolongation of one of the interior diagonals of the cube. The eye sees the outline of a regular hexagon.

In Fig. 5–11e the eye is opposite the midpoint of one of the edges. No part of the upper or lower bases is visible.

In Fig. 5–11f we are looking almost broadside on the face of a cube. In the latter two cases (and others) it becomes impossible to complete the third parallelogram. We can consider each such case as a zero parallelogram.

Symmetries of the Cube

Symmetries are of various types. They occur in both two and three dimensions. Points **A** and **B** are symmetric with respect to line l_1 if **AO** = **OB** and if the angles at **O** are right angles. This relation is usually referred to as "axial" or "bilateral" symmetry (Fig. 5–12a).

Points **A**, **B** and **C** (Fig. 5–12b) have "rotational" symmetry with respect to point **O** of the circle. If each point is advanced 120 degrees around the circle, clockwise or counterclockwise, it will occupy the position of another of the points. The symmetry discussed is a rotational symmetry of 120 degrees. Numbers associated with rotational symmetry are always exact divisors of 360 degrees.

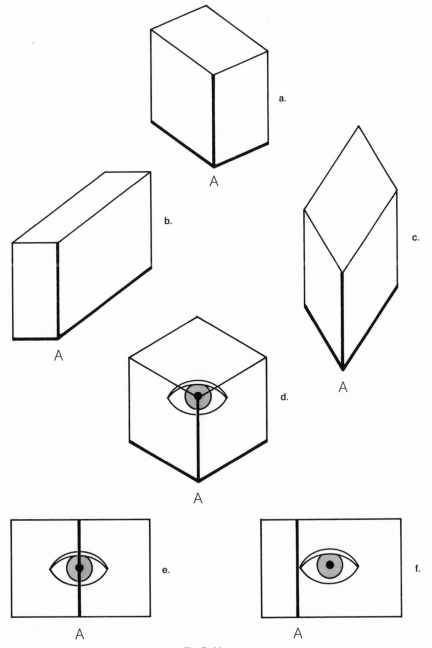

a.

b.

c.

A

A

d.

A

A

e.

f.

A

A

Fig. 5–11

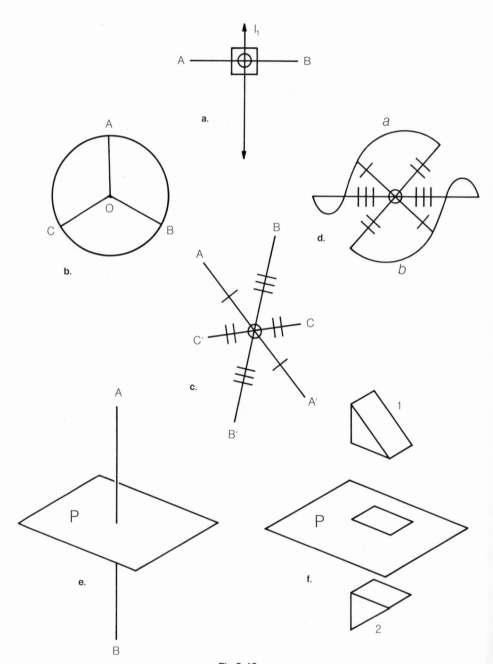

Fig. 5-12

Points A, B and C in Fig. 5–12c are "radially" symmetric with respect to point O. This is also called "central" symmetry. Radial symmetry usually involves a reverse twist. Note the reversal (Fig. 5–12d) of the two curves a and b. The curves are radially symmetric with respect to point O.

Point A is symmetric to point B with regard to plane P. The plane is the perpendicular bisector of AB (Fig. 5–12e).

Solid 1 (Fig. 5–12f) is symmetric to solid 2 with respect to plane P. A mirror image is a common example of this type of symmetry.

A cube is rich in its symmetries. There are 23 symmetries in every cube.

1. The upper half of a cube is symmetric to the lower half with respect to plane P. There are three such symmetries (Fig. 5–13a, b and c).

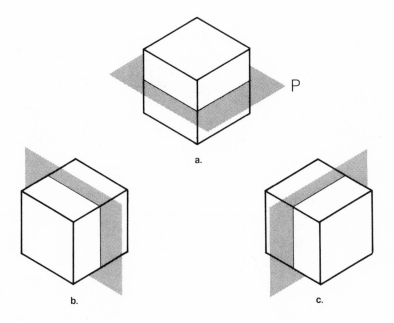

a.

b.   c.

Fig. 5–13

2. A diagonal plane of a cube separates the cube into halves that are symmetric with respect to the rectangle **ABCD** (Fig. 5–14a). There are six such symmetries (Fig. 5–14b–g).

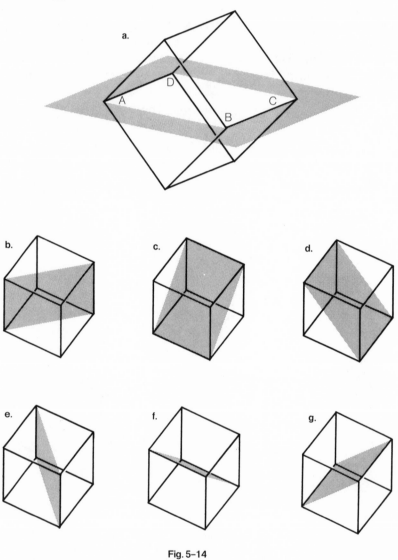

Fig. 5–14

3. A cube has a rotational symmetry of 90 degrees with respect to perpendiculars erected at the centers of each pair of parallel faces. There are three such symmetries.

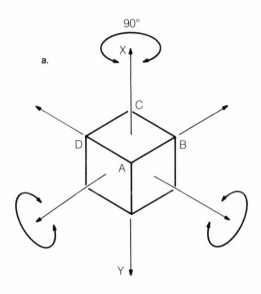

	0° or 360°	90°	180°	270°
A	A	B	C	D
B	B	C	D	A
C	C	D	Ⓐ	B
D	D	A	B	C

b.

Fig. 5–15

A succession of 90-degree rotations about an axis as in Fig. 5–15a will carry the cube back into itself. Four rotations of 90 degrees will restore the cube to its original position. Figure 5–15b summarizes the results of rotations of 90, 180, 270 and 360 degrees about the axis XY. A rotation of either

75

0 degrees or 360 degrees will produce the same result. So will rotations of $90° \pm n \cdot 360°$, $180° \pm n \cdot 360°$, and $270° \pm n \cdot 360°$ where n is a natural number (1, 2, 3, 4, . . . etc.). Once an original rotation is made, further rotations of multiples of 360 degrees will not change the final position. The cell circled in Fig. 5–15b indicates that the original vertex **C** after a rotation of 180 degrees assumes the position of **A**.

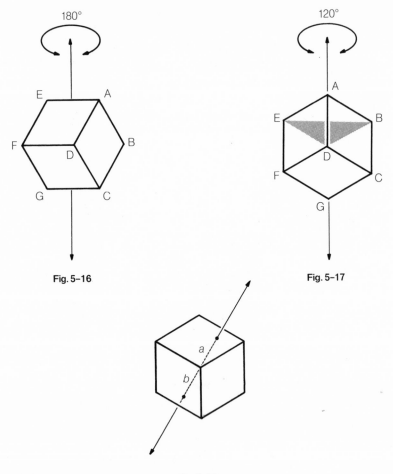

Fig. 5–16

Fig. 5–17

Fig. 5–18

4. A cube has a rotational symmetry of 180 degrees with respect to lines that join the midpoints of diagonally opposite edges of a cube. There are six such symmetries. Rotations of multiples of 180 degrees will restore the cube to its original outline in space. Rotations of an odd number of multiples of 180 degrees will change positions of lettered vertices. Rotations of an even number of multiples of 180 degrees will restore the vertices to their original position (Fig. 5–16).

5. A cube has a rotational symmetry of 120 degrees with respect to the interior diagonals of the cube. There are four such symmetries. Rotations of 120 degrees will carry the cube back into itself. This occurs because axis **AG** is perpendicular to the plane of triangle **BDE** at its center. This triangle is equilateral, since its sides are diagonals of the congruent faces of the original cube. Rotations of $3n \times 120°$ will carry vertices back to their original positions (n is a natural number) (Fig. 5–17).

6. If any line is drawn through the center of a cube, the segments cut off by the surface of the cube (*e.g., a* and *b* in Fig. 5–18) are always equal. Thus the center of a cube is a point of central symmetry.

Of its 23 symmetries, therefore, a cube contains:

1 symmetry with respect to a point;
9 symmetries with respect to a plane;
13 symmetries with respect to a line.

Surface Geodesics

A geodesic is the shortest distance between two points. Let us now consider the geodesics of a cube, restricting ourselves to the surface of the cube. This is said to be our domain. There are three basic cases, of which the third case has a number of subcases.

Case 1. Points **A** and **B** lie on the same face of the cube (Fig. 5–19). The geodesic is plainly the segment **AB**. Its maximum length is $e\sqrt{2}$.

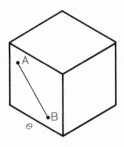

Fig. 5–19

Case 2. Points **A** and **C** lie on adjacent faces of the cube. If we flatten out the surface of the cube (Fig. 5–20a), the segment **AC** is the shortest path between the two points. When we restore the cube to its third dimension, the broken path **AXC** will be the shortest way to go from **A** to **C** (Fig. 5–20b). Its maximum length is $e\sqrt{5}$.

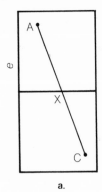

a.

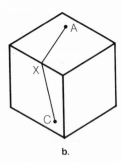

b.

Fig. 5–20

78

Case 3. Points **A** and **B** lie on opposite faces of the cube in Fig. 5–21a. Since a cube results from the intersection of three pairs of parallel planes, many such cases can arise.

Consider one of the most common ways of flattening out the surface of a cube (Fig. 5–21b). For convenience in the discussion of Case 3, Face F is being used in four different places.

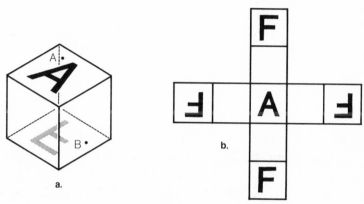

Fig. 5–21

It would be helpful to construct a paper model of a cube because the mathematics connected with this particular geodesic becomes complicated. Bear in mind that although we are picking our two points on parallel faces A and F, there are two other pairs of parallel faces which could have been used. Regardless of the pair picked, the mathematics will be identical. In addition, bear in mind that when **A** and **B** lie on opposite faces, there are four possible routes between the two points. We seek the *geodesic*. Much of the discussion of these cases depends on the specific locations of **A** and **B** within their particular squares.

Subcase 1. Here (Fig. 5–22a and b) each of the points is at the center of a face of the cube. It doesn't matter which path is taken. In all cases, the geodesic between **A** and **B** has the value 2*e*.

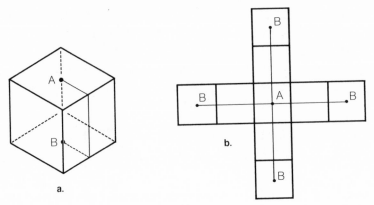

Fig. 5–22

Subcase 2. Here (Fig. 5–23a and b) one of the points, **A**, is in the center of the northeast quarter of the original square face. The opposite face of the cube has also been separated into four quarters. The second point, **B**, has been designated **B₁**, **B₂**, **B₃** and **B₄** in accordance with its position in the four quarters of the bottom square. **B** always lies at the center of its quarter-square. Since any corner of the top face of the cube can be reoriented to the northeast position, our procedure should take care of all possible relations of

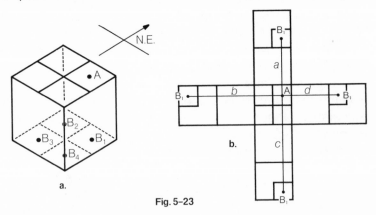

Fig. 5–23

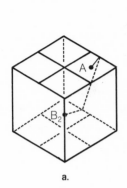

a.

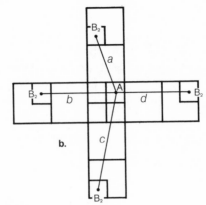

b.

Fig. 5-24

top-bottom points. An analysis of Fig. 5–23b using B_1 as the bottom point shows the values:

$a = 1^1/_2 e$
$b = 2^1/_2 e$
$c = 2^1/_2 e$
$d = 1^1/_2 e$

The geodesic here is obviously path a or d.

Subcase 3. Here (Fig. 5–24a) point **A** is still in the center of the northeast quarter of the original square. Point **B** is in position B_2. Analysis of Fig. 5–24b shows the values:

$$a = \frac{\sqrt{10}}{2} = 1.581e$$

$$b = 2e$$

$$c = \frac{\sqrt{26}}{2} = 2.550e$$

$$d = 2e$$

The Pythagorean theorem provides solutions when a slanted distance has to be found. The geodesic is path a.

Subcase 4. Another possibility (Fig. 5–25a) exists with reference to the position of the two points **A** and **B**. Point **B** is . in position **B₃**. Interestingly, all four distances in this case are alike (Fig. 5–25b). Any of the four could be considered the geodesic. In this case, it doesn't matter which face of the cube we go down. This is reminiscent of the problem: If you are at the center of a circle, what would be the shortest route from the center to a point on the circumference?

Subcase 5. Figure 5–25c shows that the value of *a* in this case is 2.062*e*. This is a repetition of Subcase 3. Here we

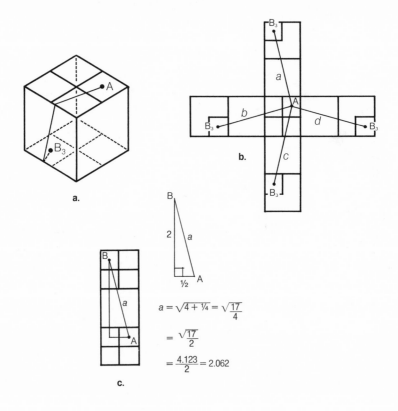

$$a = \sqrt{4 + \tfrac{1}{4}} = \sqrt{\tfrac{17}{4}}$$

$$= \frac{\sqrt{17}}{2}$$

$$= \frac{4.123}{2} = 2.062$$

c.

Fig. 5–25

would be discussing the relation between A and B_4 (Fig. 5–26). This is identical to the relation between A and B_2 in Subcase 3. Points B_2 and B_4 are symmetric with reference to point A. Relations will be no different from what they were.

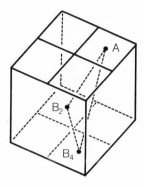

Fig. 5–26

Solution of the geodesic between points on opposite faces of a cube is by no means complete. Consider Fig. 5–27a. When points A and B_1 were at the centers of respective quarter-squares, either route was acceptable. When A and B_1 do not lie at the centers of quarter-squares (Fig. 5–27b), the best we can do is determine the geodesics by use of the Pythagorean theorem. We must now know how far points A and B_1 are from the edges of their respective quarter-squares. The distances for A are w and x, and y and z are these distances for B_1. These calculations are carried out in Fig. 5–27b.

Let us, finally, consider the case in which we begin with a point on any face of a cube. We wish to start at a point, P, visit every face of the cube and return to P again (Fig. 5–28a). Hugo Steinhaus, in his admirable book *Mathematical Snapshots,* likens this to the case of the spider who wishes to search each face for a possible fly. How can this be done most economically? We can, of course, wander at random over the six faces and then return home, but what we seek is the *geodesic*. Consider one of the many possible patterns of the surfaces of a cube (there are eleven of these patterns (Fig. 5–28b). Add a repeated face, for convenience in calculation. Connect point **P** with its repeated position. If we were to go from **P** to **P'** on a plane by the shortest route, we would certainly know how to do this. Since the straight segment is the geodesic between two points on a plane, path **PP'** must be the solution to our problem. If **QQ'** is exam-

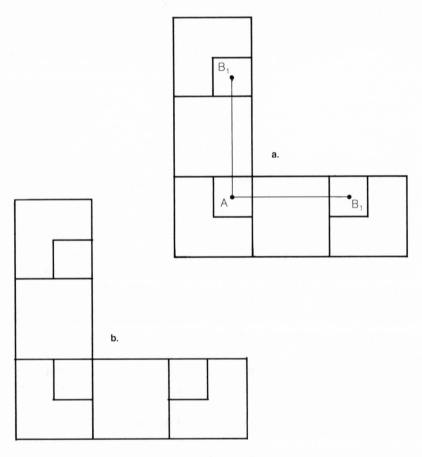

Fig. 5–27

ined, it will reveal that the geodesic is always of constant length no matter where we begin on the surface of the cube. The proof of this is beyond the scope of this book. The length of this geodesic is always $3e\sqrt{2}$. This is the length of **RR'**, the hypotenuse of a right triangle with legs of length $3e$. The figure **STUVWX–S** (Fig. 5–28c) is a par-hexagon; its opposite sides are parallel by pairs. It can also be shown that $a + a' = b + b' = c + c' = e\sqrt{2}$.

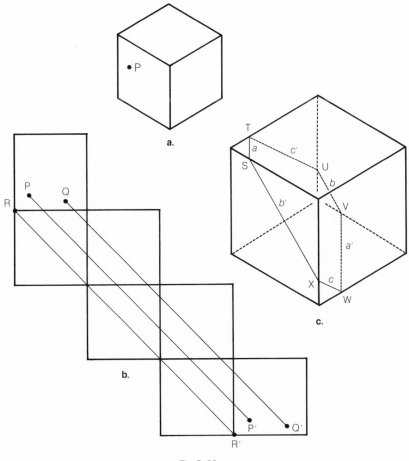

Fig. 5–28

CHAPTER VI
Games with Cubes

It might have crossed your mind that a chapter on games with cubes would be about dice games. Dice games are certainly games with cubes, but what we have in mind are games of a more mathematical nature.

We begin with some adventures in the visualization of space. Figure 6–1 shows eight different groupings of cubes with marked faces. In any one group, all the cubes are alike. The game is to decide, by looking at a particular group, how the sides are marked and how the markings are oriented with respect to one another on the unit cube.

Prince Rupert's Cube

Suppose that a square channel is bored through a wooden cube (Fig. 6–2a). Evidently a second cube, with edges slightly smaller than the width of the hole, could be pushed

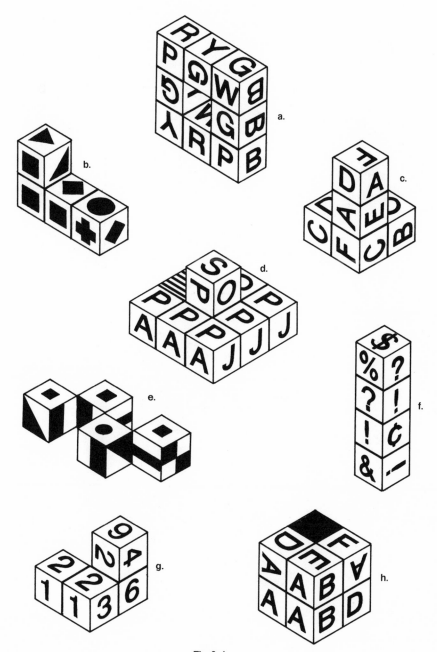

Fig. 6–1

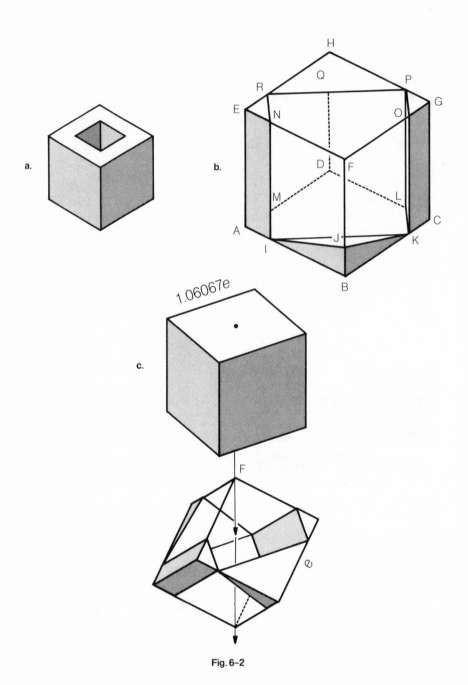

a.

b.

c.

1.06067*e*

Fig. 6–2

through the channel. If the width of the channel is increased, larger cubes can be pushed through these holes. If the size of the square channel approaches the width of the original cube, there is the danger that the original cube will disappear. The original cube is **ABCDEFGH** (Fig. 6–2b).

Now suppose we try to imagine a square channel bored through the cube at some angle so as to accommodate the largest possible cube. Strangely enough, it can be shown that a cube larger than the original can be pushed through the cube. True, it won't be *much* larger—its edge can be about 1.06067 times the edge of the original, but still it is larger. If you examine Fig. 6–2b and c you will see how this is done. (**AM = AI = BJ = KC = CL = GO = GP = HQ = ER = EN =** 1/4 edge of the original cube.) If this channel is cut out, it can't be quite 1.06067 times the length of the original edge. Better make it just 1.06066—then maybe the cube won't disintegrate. Come to think of it, we'd better make the edge of the cube we pass through only 1.06065. It will fit better.

~~Soma Blocks~~

STEINHAUS (OR MIKOWSKI) CUBES

~~Soma Blocks, invented by the Danish mathematician Piet Hein,~~ are the six groups of blocks shown in Fig. 6–3. Each group is composed of the number of cubes indicated. They are obtainable commercially. Since the sum of the volumes of the six groups is 27 cubic units, it is readily apparent that the blocks in the six groups *could,* possibly, be assembled into a cube three units on a side. The difficulty is doing it.

The Cube as a Factoring Lattice

Figures 6–4a and b look as though they are outlines of cubes. They are not meant to be. They are lattices, or two-

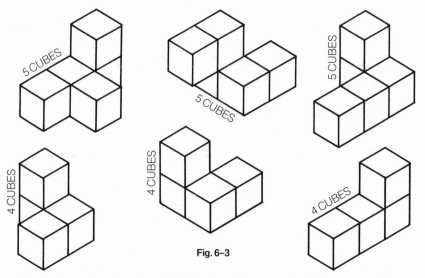

Fig. 6–3

dimensional networks, that indicate possible integral factors of the numbers 30 and 105.

In Fig. 6–4a start at the number 1 and trace any continuous network that terminates at the number 30. All the possible orders of the prime factors of 30 will be encountered—neglecting alternative orderings based on varying placements of the factor 1. At a given point on any chosen path, the next factor is determined by finding the number which, when multiplied by the given point, produces a value equal to that of the next point. Thus, the path illustrated proceeds from point 1 through points 2 and 6 to 30. The set of factors arrived at is then: $1 \times 2 \times 3 \times 5$. Locate all the other possible orders: $1 \times 2 \times 5 \times 3$, $1 \times 3 \times 2 \times 5$, $1 \times 3 \times 5 \times 2$, $1 \times 5 \times 2 \times 3$, $1 \times 5 \times 3 \times 2$.

The lattice in Fig. 6–4b illustrates the possible factors of 105; its prime factors are $3 \times 5 \times 7$, with the 1 included for convenience in starting the path. Illustrated by the arrows is the order $1 \times 5 \times 3 \times 7$. See whether you can locate all the other possible orders of factors.

The whole principle of the lattice depends upon obtaining the prime factors of the original natural number. Note that

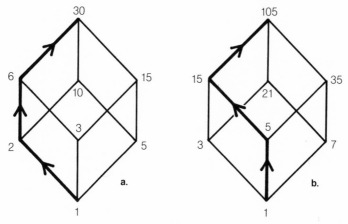

Fig. 6–4

the first row 2, 3, 5 in Fig. 6–4a uses the factors one at a time. The second row 6, 10, 15 uses these factors two at a time. A third row would use the factors of the first row three at a time, etc.

The lattice in Fig. 6–5a, organized around the outline of a cube, may be used to indicate the relations among the primary colors. Start at the bottom, at symbol ϕ. This may be used to signify the absence of color. The first horizontal row indicates the introduction of the primary colors—red, yellow and blue. Mixtures of these primaries, two at a time, bring about the binary colors—orange, purple and green. At the very top we have white—the theoretical color produced by the mixture of red, yellow and blue. The path traced is an indication that ϕ is present in Red, which is present in Orange, which is present in White.

The lattice in Fig. 6–5b indicates a similar structure but in the field of set theory. Start at the bottom. The null or empty set is an element of **A**, **B**, or **C**. When these elements are combined two at a time, the next row appears. At the very top we have a set that contains three elements. The path traced indicates that the null set is a subset of **A**, which is a subset of **AC**, which is a subset of the set containing **ABC**.

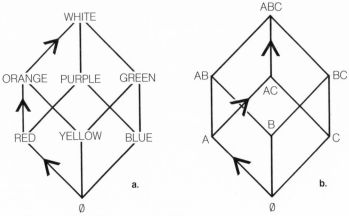

Fig. 6–5

The Cube and Probability

The next few pages presuppose some knowledge of combinations and probability. Within the field of combinations, it is presumed that the reader knows that the number of ways 3 things can be selected from a collection of 7 things is $_7C_3$ or $\binom{7}{3}$ (where C stands for the number of combinations of elements.) Its value is: $\dfrac{7 \times 6 \times 5}{1 \times 2 \times 3} = 35$

The value of $_8C_2$ is: $\dfrac{8 \times 7}{1 \times 2} = 28$

Certainty, in probability, is represented by the number 1. Impossibility is represented by the number 0.

As far as we know, the probability that a human being will ultimately die is 1.

The probability of tossing a common die and obtaining a 7 is 0. At least it is 0 with an honest die.

Calculating the probability of a certain outcome consists in finding the ratio of the number of ways in which that outcome can occur to the total number of outcomes. *For example:* If we neglect leap years, the probability that a person was born on the 4th of July is 1/365.

If I am thinking of a particular face of a die, the probability that you will guess this face is 1/6. This means that, on the average, if you try this particular experiment 600 times, you will be successful, in general, about 100 times.

If I am thinking of a particular edge of a cube, the probability that you will guess this edge is 1/12.

Distances between the eight distinct vertices of a cube can be of three lengths:

1. e, the length of the side of the cube;
2. $e\sqrt{2}$, the length of the face diagonal of the cube;
3. $e\sqrt{3}$, the length of the interior diagonal of the cube.

If two vertices of a cube are selected at random, what is the probability that the distance between them is: at least e, at least $e\sqrt{2}$, at least $e\sqrt{3}$, or more than $e\sqrt{3}$?

The probability that the distance between vertices is at least e will be 1. This means that it is certain.

The probability that the distance between vertices is at least $e\sqrt{2}$ is 16/28, or 4/7. Both $e\sqrt{2}$ and $e\sqrt{3}$ lengths must be considered.

At least $e\sqrt{3}$	4/28, or 1/7
More than e	16/28, or 4/7
More than $e\sqrt{2}$	4/28, or 1/7
More than $e\sqrt{3}$	0, which is impossible.

The chart in Fig. 6–6a shows the distances between each possible pair of distinct vertices and may help in working out the probabilities.

Coloring Cubes

Problems concerning the coloring of cubes offer interesting possibilities for investigation. There is only one cube with six black faces. No matter how it is rotated, it always looks

	A	B	C	D	C	F	G	H
A	0	e	$e\sqrt{2}$	e	e	$e\sqrt{2}$	$e\sqrt{3}$	$e\sqrt{2}$
B	e	0	e	$e\sqrt{2}$	$e\sqrt{2}$	e	$e\sqrt{2}$	$e\sqrt{3}$
C	$e\sqrt{2}$	e	0	e	$e\sqrt{3}$	$e\sqrt{2}$	e	$e\sqrt{2}$
D	e	$e\sqrt{2}$	e	0	$e\sqrt{2}$	$e\sqrt{3}$	$e\sqrt{2}$	e
E	e	$e\sqrt{2}$	$e\sqrt{3}$	$e\sqrt{2}$	0	e	$e\sqrt{2}$	e
F	$e\sqrt{2}$	e	$e\sqrt{2}$	$e\sqrt{2}$	e	0	e	$e\sqrt{2}$
G	$e\sqrt{3}$	$e\sqrt{2}$	e	$e\sqrt{2}$	$e\sqrt{2}$	e	0	e
H	$e\sqrt{2}$	$e\sqrt{3}$	$e\sqrt{2}$	e	e	$e\sqrt{2}$	e	0

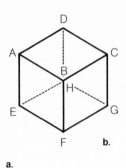

a.

b.

Fig. 6-6

the same. If you were trying to place it in all possible positions, or orientations, you would never know when you were repeating a position. Let us examine the coloring problem more thoroughly by listing the possible colorings of a cube when two colors, black and white, are available.

There is only one all-white cube. We shall refer to it as a W_6B_0 type. This abbreviation will be used for a cube with six white surfaces (no black surfaces). There is but one all-black cube. We can call it the W_0B_6 type.

The listing of the other possibilities must include: W_5B_1, W_4B_2, W_3B_3, W_2B_4, W_1B_5. Because the arrangements are symmetric, the problem is easier than it looks. When we solve the W_5B_1 situation, we can establish W_1B_5 by merely exchanging black for white.

Let us now consider the various combinations.

W_5B_1. There is but one cube of this type. No matter which face is black, it can always be placed at the top (Fig. 6–7a).

W_1B_5. There is but one of this type (Fig. 6–7b).

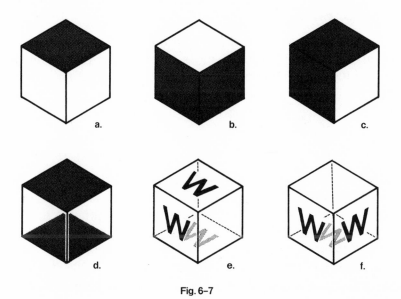

Fig. 6–7

W_4B_2. Two black surfaces can exist but in two different ways (Fig. 6–7c and d).

The remaining faces must be white. We have now established the existence of two types of the W_4B_2 and two types of the W_2B_4 types.

Three white surfaces may exist in but two ways. In the first of the possibilities (Fig. 6–7e) the three surfaces are adjoining; two of the three are parallel. In the second case (Fig. 6–7f) the three surfaces come together at one of the corners of the cube. In both cases it is possible to complete the coloring in but one way. We have now established the existence of two W_3B_3 types of cube colorations.

By referring to the W_4B_2 solution previously determined, we can establish the existence of two of the W_2B_4 types. There will be but one of the W_1B_5 types and but one of the W_0B_6 types.

To summarize, the coloring of a cube with the two colors white and black can be accomplished in but 10 ways:

Pattern: W_0B_6 W_1B_5 W_2B_4 W_3B_3 W_4B_2 W_5B_1 W_6B_0
No. of ways: 1   1   2   2   2   1   1

You may be interested in experimentation with the coloration of cubes with three or more colors. If you eventually arrive at the six-color problem, you'll have real trouble on your hands.

Cube Cutting

Imagine a cube made of wood and painted red on its six faces. Imagine that we are to slice the cube in such a manner as to cut it into one-inch cubes. If we begin with a cube $1 \times 1 \times 1$, we obviously need no cuts. A cube $2 \times 2 \times 2$ (Fig. 6–8) will require three cuts—two vertically, at right angles to each other, and one horizontally. A cube $3 \times 3 \times 3$ will require six cuts—four vertically, at right angles to each other, and two horizontally.

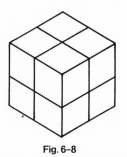

Fig. 6–8

Since just the outside of these cubes was painted red, some of the smaller $1 \times 1 \times 1$ cubes will have more red faces than the others. Figure 6–9 summarizes the statistics with reference to cubes of different sizes. Finally, we generalize for a cube e units on a side.

This table presents some interesting aspects when percentage considerations are involved.

96

For example, in the cube $1 \times 1 \times 1$, 100 percent of the cubes are of the R_6W_0 type.

In the cube $2 \times 2 \times 2$, 100 percent of the cubes are of the R_3W_3 type.

In the cube $3 \times 3 \times 3$, the percentage composition is as follows:

R_3W_3 29.6 R_2W_4 44.4 R_1W_5 22.2 R_0W_6 3.7

Size of cube	No. of cuts to produce $1 \times 1 \times 1$ cube	No. of $1 \times 1 \times 1$ cubes	No. of R_6W_0 cubes	No. of R_5W_1 cubes	No. of R_4W_2 cubes	No. of R_3W_3 cubes	No. of R_2W_4 cubes	No. of R_1W_1 cubes	No. of R_0W_6 cubes
$1 \times 1 \times 1$	0	1	1	0	0	0	0	0	0
$2 \times 2 \times 2$	3	8	0	0	0	8	0	0	0
$3 \times 3 \times 3$	6	27	0	0	0	8	12	6	1
$4 \times 4 \times 4$	9	64	0	0	0	8	24	24	8
$5 \times 5 \times 5$	12	125	0	0	0	8	36	54	27
$e \times e \times e$	$3(e-1)$	e^3	0	0	0	8	$12(e-2)$	$6(e-2)^2$	$(e-2)^3$

R = exterior faces
W = interior faces

Fig. 6–9

Figure 6–10 summarizes percentage compositions for cubes with sides ranging from two to ten units.

Many curious relationships can be detected in these statistics:

Composition of Cubes with Various Exposures by Percent				
Side of Cube	R_3W_3	R_2W_4	R_1W_5	R_0W_6
2	$\frac{8}{8}=100\%$	0	0	0
3	$\frac{8}{27}=29.6\%$	$\frac{12}{27}=44.4\%$	$\frac{6}{27}=22.2\%$	$\frac{1}{27}=3.7\%$
4	$\frac{8}{64}=12.5\%$	$\frac{27}{64}=37.5\%$	$\frac{24}{64}=37.5\%$	$\frac{8}{64}=12.5\%$
5	$\frac{8}{125}=6.4\%$	$\frac{36}{125}=28.8\%$	$\frac{54}{125}=43.2\%$	$\frac{27}{125}=21.6\%$
6	$\frac{8}{216}=3.7\%$	$\frac{48}{216}=22.2\%$	$\frac{96}{216}=44.4\%$	$\frac{64}{216}=29.6\%$
7	$\frac{8}{343}=2.3\%$	$\frac{60}{343}=17.5\%$	$\frac{150}{343}=43.7\%$	$\frac{125}{343}=36.4\%$
8	$\frac{8}{512}=1.6\%$	$\frac{72}{512}=14.0\%$	$\frac{216}{512}=42.2\%$	$\frac{216}{512}=42.2\%$
9	$\frac{8}{729}=1.1\%$	$\frac{84}{729}=11.5\%$	$\frac{294}{729}=40.3\%$	$\frac{343}{729}=47.0\%$
10	$\frac{8}{1000}=0.8\%$	$\frac{96}{1000}=9.6\%$	$\frac{384}{1000}=38.4\%$	$\frac{512}{1000}=51.2\%$

Fig. 6–10

1. In every case exactly eight cubes have the exposure R_3W_3. This is called an "invariant"—a statistic or phenomenon in mathematics that never changes. It is violated only when the cube has an edge one unit long. Note that the R_3W_3 entries dwindle from 100 percent down to 0.8 percent. The value approaches zero as the number of units on a side increases.

2. Column 2, R_2W_4 entries, decreases constantly.

3. Column 3, R_1W_5 entries, shows an interesting progres-

sion. The percentages increase up to a maximum of 44.4 percent, then start to decrease.

4. Column 4, R_0W_6 entries, increases from the very beginning and never stops increasing.

Note also the following curious features:

1. The entries for edge 3 and edge 6 are exactly the same but in reverse order.

2. When the side of the cube is 8, both R_1W_5 and R_0W_6 have the same percentage compositions. From that point on, the R_1W_6 values always exceed the R_1W_5 values.

3. When the side of the cube is 4, the entries have an interesting symmetry: 12.5 percent, 37.5 percent, 37.5 percent and 12.5 percent.

4. In order to get some idea of what will happen when the side of the cube is made quite large, let us select a length of 102 units. The composition then becomes:

R_3W_3	$8/1,061,208 = 0.00075\%$
R_2W_4	$1200/1,061,208 = 0.113\%$
R_1W_5	$60,000/1,061,208 = 5.65\%$
R_0W_6	$1,000,000/1,061,208 = 94.2\%$

As the cube becomes larger, or as the faces of a unit cube are subdivided more and more, the R_0W_6 cubes increase in percentage and approach closer and closer to some terminal figure.

Crazy Cubes, or Instant Insanity

Make four cubes and color the faces as shown in Fig. 6–11a–d: W(hite), R(ed), B(lue), Y(ellow). These cubes are the objects you need for playing "Crazy Cubes." You have only to place the cubes in a row so that all the faces are a different color on the top row, bottom row, and both side rows.

Figure 6–12a seems to show that the problem is solved,

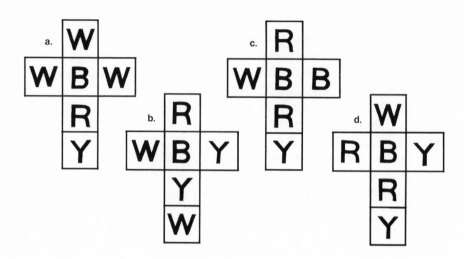

Fig. 6–11

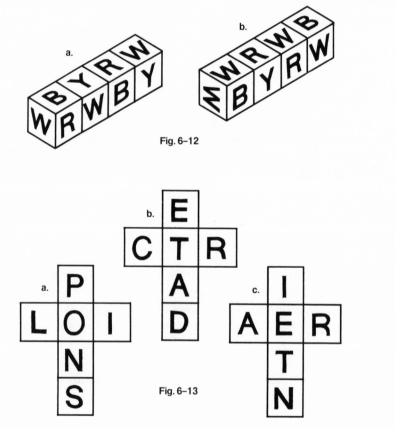

Fig. 6–12

Fig. 6–13

but turn the whole row toward you. Now it looks like Fig. 6–12b, and the colors on the top row are *not* all different.

Keep trying!

Spelling and the Cube

The pattern in Fig. 6–13a is to be folded into a cube. Start at any of the faces. Proceed from that face to an adjacent one and see how many words you can spell. You may return to a face you have just left. In the pattern illustrated, the following words can be obtained: ONIONS, SNIP, PINS, SLOP, IONS, LOP, SPIN, NIPS, LOINS, OPINIONS.

What is the longest word you can form from those that can be selected from the cube in Fig. 6–13b? Typical word: DE-TRACTED.

Try the same thing with the cube in Fig. 6–13c. Typical word: RETREATER.

CHAPTER VII
Curiosities of the Cube

This entire book, as its title indicates, is about curiosities of the cube. We have saved some of the most unusual facts about cubes for this concluding chapter.

Hamiltonian Routes and Unicursal Routes on the Cube

Suppose that a bug who lives at vertex **A** decides to visit his cousins who live at **B**, **C**, **D**, **E**, **F**, **G** and **H**. Suppose, furthermore, that he decides to visit each cousin once and only once. He could traverse the path indicated by the heavy lines in Fig. 7–1a. There would be many such possible routes.

Such a route is called a Hamiltonian Route. It is named after the British mathematician William Rowan Hamilton, one of the first mathematicians to investigate the field. At present his work would be considered part of network theory. The Hamiltonian Route is more easily traversed via the rabbatment outlined in Fig. 7–1b. Figure 7–1a and 7–1b outline the same route: A–E–F–G–H–D–C–B. Note that the route requires but seven segments. This is one fewer than the number of vertices of the cube. In general, the Hamiltonian Route is always one less than the number of vertices.

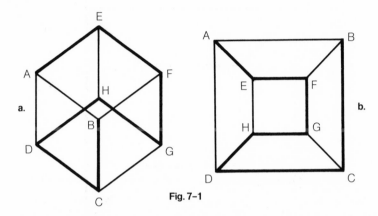

Fig. 7–1

The Unicursal Route, or Euler Path, is named after the Swiss mathematician Leonhard Euler, who made vital contributions to all branches of mathematics. This route seeks to trace out each of the edges of a solid without repetition. It cannot always be done. Fig. 7–2 indicates a distortion of the twelve edges of the cube. Distortion or not, the network repeats the actual connections of vertices that occur in the cube. A traverse of the 12 edges requires four separate routes. The first begins at B and covers the path B–F–E–A–B–C–G–H–D–C. Then separate routes take care of AD, EH and FG.

There is an extensive literature on both the Hamiltonian Route and the Unicursal Route. Some writers on the subject call the first the Salesman's Route, after a salesman who wishes to visit each and every town in his territory once and only once. The other may be called the Inspector's Route, referring to an inspector who has to inspect all the roads in his territory. If it were possible to visit each road once and only once, he would be happy. Unfortunately, this is not always possible. Each of the two problems has its own rules. One is not to be confused with the other.

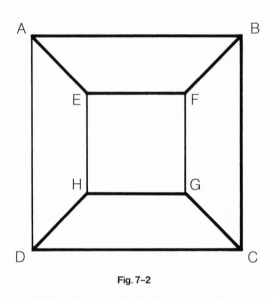

Fig. 7–2

Duplicating the Cube

A famous story about a cube concerns the inhabitants of the ancient Greek community of Delos who were being visited with a plague for which there seemed to be no cure. The oracle, who was consulted for a way to appease Apollo, instructed them to build a cubical altar exactly double the volume of the present one. The Delians thought they had obeyed the instruction when they constructed an altar having an edge double the length of the original edge. The plague continued. The volume of the new altar was not double that of the old one but eight times its size!

The construction that the oracle ordered is impossible if the edge is to be laid out with an unmarked straightedge and compass, and these were the tools of the period for such a task. If the oracle had not specified the shape of the altar, would the rhombic dodecahedron have had the required volume?

Shadow Pictures

When is a cube not a cube? Never, but the shadow of a cube may seem not to have come from a cube. In order to make shadows, you need a light source and a screen. The light source may be sunlight, a flashlight or an unshaded lightbulb; the screen may be a piece of white paper, a wall or a sheet over the back of a chair.

If a line constructed from the center of the light source is perpendicular to both the screen and a face of the cube, the shadow is a square. The shadow is called the projection of the object, in this case the cube. It consists of a polygon and all the points of its interior.

Move the cube slowly about and watch the change in its projection. Before you try this experiment, decide whether the polygon will ever have more than four sides. If it will, what is the greatest number of sides it will have? What is the least number? There should be some relation between this experiment and the straw cube of Fig. 2–10 on page 15.

Answer the same questions for shadows of the space dual of the cube, the octahedron. If you did the construction on page 20, you have one of these.

Caution: To keep your fingers out of the shadow, push a piece of stiff wire between two opposite vertices of the figure to be projected, leaving the ends long enough for holding.

Instead of moving the cube, you can keep it stationary and move the light source.

Measurements of the Cube

There are many interesting exercises related to the three most common measures associated with the cube. Recall that:

The volume of a cube is found through the formula:

$$V = e^3$$

The surface area of the six faces of a cube is found through the formula:

$$A = 6e^2$$

The measure of the twelve edges of a cube is found through the formula:

$$P = 12e$$

Try your hand at the following:

1. The total surface area of a cube has the same number of units of measure as the volume. What is the length of the edge?

2. The volume of a cube has the same number of units of measure as the perimeter of all the edges. What is the length of the edge?

3. The total surface area of a cube has the same number of units of measure as the perimeter of all the edges. What is the length of the edge?

4. Is it possible to discover a cube in which the total surface area, volume and perimeter of all edges have the same measure?

Certain calculations with respect to the cube can be interrelated with those of the cone, cylinder, etc. The following formulas will come in handy:

Volume of a right circular cone $= (^1/_3)\pi r^2 h$
Volume of a right circular cylinder $= \pi r^2 h$
Total surface area of a right circular cylinder $= 2\pi rh + 2\pi r^2$
Volume of a sphere $= (^4/_3)\pi r^3$
Surface of a sphere $= 4\pi r^2$

The Hypercube

A cube in four dimensions is called a hypercube or tesseract. This cube we cannot visualize in our three-dimensional minds. However, we know a lot about it. For instance: just as we know that our familiar cube has 8 vertices, 12 edges and 6 faces, we can draw the conclusion that the hypercube has 16 vertices, 32 edges, 24 faces and 8 volumes. Let us see why:

Suppose we call the world of zero dimension that of the point. It has the property of location. If that point can move out of its one-dimensional world and reproduce itself, it leaves a trail called a line which has the new property of length. This world is the world of one dimension. Whenever a move is made from one dimension to another, a new property is added or taken away.

If a line can move out of its one-dimensional world and reproduce itself, it leaves a trail called a surface which has the property of area. This world is the world of two dimensions. Now if a surface can move out of its two-dimensional world and reproduce itself, it leaves a trail called a solid which has the property of volume. This world is the world of three dimensions. Here the argument proceeds to the world of four dimensions. If a solid could move out of its three-dimensional world and reproduce itself, it would leave a trail called a hypersolid which has the property of content.

To approach the hypercube suppose we start with a point. Let the point move a given distance in the direction which we feel is straight. The point has reproduced itself and at the same time has generated "something between" which we will call length. This one-dimensional figure is called a line segment. Let this line segment move in a direction perpendicular to itself and a length equal to itself. The line segment has reproduced itself and generated "something between" which we call area. This two-dimensional figure is called a square. Likewise if the square moves in a direction perpendicular to itself and a distance equal to the line segment, the square has reproduced itself and generated "something between" which we call volume. This three-dimensional figure is called a cube. So far we can visualize every step of the way, but let us take the argument a step further. If the cube could move in a direction perpendicular to itself (whatever that may be) and a distance equal to that of the line segment, it would have reproduced itself and generated "something between" which mathematicians call content. This four-dimensional figure would be called a hypercube.

Perhaps an algebraic approach will increase our understanding. When a point, P, moves out of its zero-dimensional world, it reproduces itself while generating "something between," L. If we let an arrow represent the word "produces," then symbolically P→2P+L (Fig. 7–3a).

When this line segment, L, moves out of its one-dimensional world, it reproduces itself while generating "something between," A. So L→2L+A. However, *each* end point as well as L reproduces itself so L→2(2P+L)+ (2L+A)=4P+2L+2L+A=4P+4L+A. See how this expression indicates the square with its 4 vertices, 4 edges and an area (Fig. 7–3b).

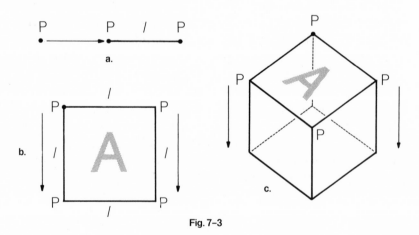

Fig. 7–3

108

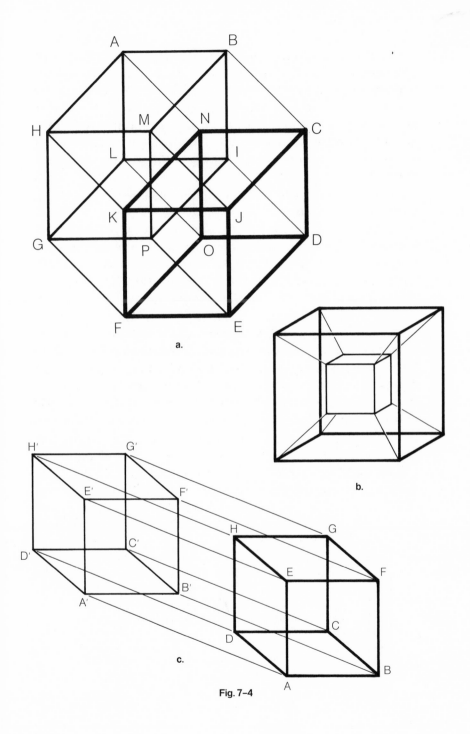

a.

b.

c.

Fig. 7-4

In like manner when the square moves out of its two-dimensional world, it reproduces itself while generating "something between," V. So A→2A + V. But now there are 4 points, 4 line segments and an area doing the reproducing, or A→4(2P + L) + 4(2L + A) + (2A + V) = 8P + 4L + 8L + 4A + 2A + V = 8P + 12L + 6A + V. This expression indicates the cube with its 8 vertices, 12 edges, 6 faces and a volume (Fig. 7–3c).

Finally, when this cube moves out of its three-dimensional world, it should reproduce itself while generating "something between," T. V→2V + T. The 8 points, 12 edges, 6 surfaces and the volume are all reproducing, or V→8(2P + L) + 12(2L + A) + 6(2A + V) + (2V + T) = 16P + 8L + 24L + 12A + 12A + 6V + 2V + T = 16P + 32L + 24A + 8V + T. This expression indicates the hypercube with its 16 vertices, 32 edges, 24 faces, 8 volumes and a content. Three of its possible representations are shown in Fig. 7–4a, b and c.

On paper which is two-dimensional, figures composed of points, lines and area can be drawn without distortion. Right angles will remain right angles. When drawing three-dimensional objects in two dimensions, something must be distorted. You have no trouble recognizing a cube when you see the drawing in Fig. 7–5a. The only actual right angles, however, are those of the faces at the front and back. Do you recognize a cube in the representation of Fig. 7–5b? Think of looking down into a box from a point directly over

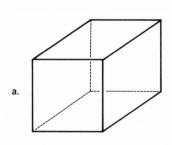

a.

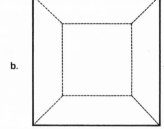

b.

Fig. 7–5

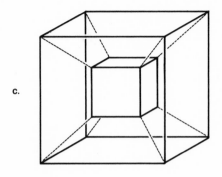

Fig. 7–5

it. Again the only actual right angles are those at the top and bottom.

You know that at each vertex of a cube, three edges are perpendicular to each other. At each vertex of a hypercube, four edges must be in that relation even though we cannot understand how this can be. Each face of the cube must become a cube in the fourth dimension. Recall that the hypercube must have 8 volumes. The original cube must reproduce itself, too. See a two-dimensional representation of the hypercube (Fig. 7–5c) and count its parts.

You might want to construct a three-dimensional version of this representation of the hypercube. Then you would be able to see the three-dimensional "shadow" of the four-dimensional hypercube even though the figure itself is beyond our comprehension.

The authors hope you will never look at a cube again and see only a cube. Perhaps you will have been stimulated to investigate other geometric figures—how they are put together and taken apart, for instance. The stimulation may lead you into fields other than geometry, too. In other words, perhaps CURIOSITIES OF THE CUBE will have made you curious about all sorts of things and stir you to investigations of your own.

About the Authors

Ernest Ranucci and Wilma Rollins shared ideas in mathematics from the time they met at a summer institute for mathematics teachers in 1956.

Mr. Ranucci's particular interest in mathematics was space perception. He taught mathematics in eighteen different countries to students in grades from kindergarten up to the university level. He was on the faculty of the State University of New York at Albany.

Mrs. Rollins taught mathematics for many years in both high school and college. She has also taught a program on television for high school students who are gifted in mathematics. She now lives in Sanford, Maine.

About the Illustrator

Henry Roth is a photographer-painter. He has produced television commercials, and both produced and directed an educational film for New York's Joffrey Ballet.

Mr. Roth was born in Cleveland, Ohio, and received his degree from the Cleveland Institute of Art. He now lives in New York City.